On *Love* and *Sex*

Born in Punjab's Hadali village (now in Pakistan) in 1915, Khushwant Singh has acquired an iconic stature: he is, arguably, India's best-known and most widely read author, columnist and journalist. He was founder-editor of *Yojana*, and editor of *The Illustrated Weekly of India*, *National Herald* and the *Hindustan Times*. His first book, *The Mark of Vishnu and Other Stories*, was published in 1950. The best known among these are the novels *Train to Pakistan*, *I Shall Not Hear the Nightingale* and *Delhi*; his autobiography, *Truth, Love and a Little Malice*; and the two-volume *A History of the Sikhs*.

Khushwant Singh was member of the Rajya Sabha from 1980 to 1986. He was awarded the Padma Bhushan in 1974; he returned the award in 1984 to protest the siege of the Golden Temple by the Indian Army. In 2007, he was awarded India's second highest civilian honour, the Padma Vibhushan.

Khushwant Singh died in 2014.

On
love
and
Sex

~SELECTED WRITINGS~

KHUSHWANT SINGH

RUPA

Published by
Rupa Publications India Pvt. Ltd 2014
7/16, Ansari Road, Daryaganj
New Delhi 110002

Sales centres:
Allahabad Bengaluru Chennai
Hyderabad Jaipur Kathmandu
Kolkata Mumbai

ISBN: 978-81-291-2493-7

10 9 8 7 6 5 4 3 2 1

First impression 2014

The moral right of the author has been asserted.

Typeset in IowanOldST BT by SÜRYA, New Delhi

Printed at Replika Press Pvt. Ltd., India

CONTENTS

MY FIRST LOVE IN COLLEGE

Some time after my matriculation results were announced, I put in an application for admission to St Stephen's College. It was then, as it is today, the most prestigious college in Delhi. At that time admissions were not as difficult as they became some years later. Boys from Modern School, coming from affluent families with a better command of English than others, were readily admitted. So was I. What I was apprehensive about was the ragging to which new entrants were subjected. It was said to be in the best tradition of British universities and designed to rub edges off boys who had fancy notions of themselves. Some of it was harmless but downright silly: asking newcomers to dance or sing, or to carry placards bearing the admission,

'I am a first-year fool'. If new entrants resisted, it could get rough. In the hostels new boys were often subjected to humiliation like being made to strip and masturbate. There had been cases when effeminate boys were subjected to buggery. I was saved from ragging by missing the first term because of prolonged illness.

In those days not much was known about typhoid. There were no blood, sputum or other tests to determine the kind of fever you had. The only medicine prescribed was a foul-smelling, bitter concoction. Solid food was forbidden. It was known to be one of a variety of miyaadi (periodical) fevers which lasted eleven or twenty-two days. If you had a relapse, you could have another bout of eleven or twenty-two days. I had two relapses. On the onset of the second, the doctors shook their heads and observed that my fate was in the hands of the Great Guru. I went into a coma. My parents had me touch trays full of rice, flour, ghee and sugar to be given away to beggars. They hired a day and a night nurse to look after me. When the battle to keep me alive seemed to have been lost, they sent for my grandmother who was then staying with my uncle at Mian Channu.

I became vaguely aware of her presence when she arrived. She took over my treatment. She tied a coloured string round the big toe of my left foot. Then she began to chant Guru Arjun's hymn Sukhmani. It went on all day and late into the night. She slept in the same room and began the chant again the next morning. By the afternoon I had come out of the coma. By the evening the fever mysteriously left me. Or perhaps it was a coincidence: the miyaad of the second twenty-two days was over.

Even before I could put my foot on the ground I was back at my pranks. I pretended to be asleep when the thermometer was slipped in my mouth and the doctor held my wrist to take my pulse. With my left hand, I quietly pressed the pulse on the inside of my elbow to stop its flow down the arm. The doctor frantically searched for my pulse, then turned up my eyelids to see if there was life in my eyes. I gave him a reassuring smile. In the three months that I spent lying in bed I gained almost two inches in height, but my liver was impaired for ever. Ever since I have slavered in the mouth while sleeping and have had to cajole my bowels into evacuating. Laxatives, purgatives and enemas became a part of my daily routine.

I had a long period of convalescence in the hills. It was pleasant to have people fussing over me, eager to do whatever I wanted. I spent two months in Shimla with my uncle and his second wife; a lovely, lotus-eyed woman who was spectacularly photogenic. It did me a world of good. I began to take long walks round Jacko Hill, ending on the Mall. It was then a most bewitching half mile of gaily lit shop windows between two highly rated restaurants, Davico's at one end, Wenger's at the other. In the centre, where four roads intersected, was Scandal Point, the place for rendezvous. Here everyone who was anyone would spend some time exchanging gossip, ogling at beautiful women and inhaling the perfumed air they left behind. You could see senior English officials, the Governor of the Punjab, the Commander-in-Chief and others, taking a stroll or on their way to the Gaiety Theatre. Every evening you saw the tall, handsome Chief Minister of the Punjab, Sir Khizr Hayat Tiwana, in his plumed turban striding ahead of his rickshaw pulled by liveried flunkies. It was hard to drag oneself away from the Mall to go home.

Those summer months in Shimla made me aware of the beauty of the Himalaya. I began to write poetry— very bad poetry. I learnt to play the sitar. I desperately wanted to fall in love with somebody, it didn't matter who or of what age, provided she was a woman. Since I could not find anyone to respond to my yearnings, I wrote anonymous love letters to a girl from Amritsar whose parents had rented the neighbouring bungalow.

I returned to Delhi and made my appearance at St Stephen's College at the beginning of the second term. The season of ragging was over. I acquired the textbooks prescribed for English literature, history, philosophy and economics. They were the most popular subjects because they were the easiest for passing examinations. I also attended Bible classes, where attendance was optional: I went to them to ingratiate myself with my Christian professors, particularly K.M. Sarkar who also taught us English literature. His stress was on the New Testament. I found the Old Testament more interesting because of the sonorous sounds of its words. I memorized passages from the *Songs of Solomon* and the *Psalms*. The *Book of Job* became my favourite reading. I sensed that in order to write good English one should be familiar with the Bible as well as European fairy tales, nursery rhymes and even nonsense verse like the limericks of Edward Lear. I read them not for fun but as the basics of literature.

My comparative affluence, generous allowance of pocket money and the fact that, like my elder brother, I had a motorcycle to ride to college, made me sought after by my classmates who were eager to be treated to free lemonades and chicken patties and ride my A.J.S. Amongst them was E.N. Mangat Rai, who was later to play a very intrusive role in my life.

His full name was Edward Nirmal Mangat Rai. He was the third child and second son of a Punjabi Hindu father who had converted to Christianity, and a Bengali Christian mother. The father was in government service and ended his career as Commissioner of Income Tax. All the four Mangat Rai children were good-looking and Westernized. The eldest, Priobala, became a college professor and retired as Principal of Kinnaird College, Lahore. She chose to remain a spinster and spent her post-retirement years in Edinburgh. The second, Charles, went into the army, married an American and retired as a Brigadier. He settled in Canada, was a yoga teacher, and on the death of his wife married a Canadian girl much younger than himself. Edward Nirmal was the third. The fourth, Sheila, was a petite, cherry-blossom beauty who made a disastrous marriage with Arthur S. Lall of the I.C.S. She bore him a daughter, Tookie, who died of cancer in her thirties in California. After divorcing Arthur, Sheila took to the bottle and drugs. She lived with a succession of lovers before she returned to India to look after her apple orchard in Kullu. She was murdered by her own servants. I mention the Mangat Rais and the Lalls because all of them re-emerged in my life at different periods.

E.N., as I called him, and I hit it off as soon as we

met. Though tall, he was somewhat effeminate. Effeminate boys were drawn towards me, perhaps because of my uncouth, rugged exterior. What initially drew me to E.N. were his academic achievements and his iconoclasm. He was much the best student in the class and usually got the top position in all the subjects in term examinations. On annual prize-distribution days, his haul of presentation books and cups made an impressive pile. He was also a good conversationalist. He questioned every assumption and accepted norm of religion and social conduct. He cleared many cobwebs from the minds of boys brought up on traditional ideas and acquired a large number of admirers, among whom I was one. We began to argue like him and imitate his manner of speech. That he preferred my friendship to that of others flattered my vanity. We were always together in class and on the sports grounds. He often spent his weekends in my home. It was wrongly assumed that our relationship was unnatural. However, Principal S.N. Mukherjee leant an ear to gossip and forbade Rai from leaving the hostel on holidays.

My two years at St Stephen's opened up an India I had not known in the enclosed atmosphere of Modern School. There were men with strange names like Sarkar, which meant government. Despite having spent the first few years of my life in a predominantly Muslim village, and given my admiration for my Urdu teacher, Moulvi Shafiuddin Nayyar, I was pained to discover that most Muslims in college regarded themselves as a community apart from other Indians. At that time the nationalist movement was on the upsurge. Gandhi had become the Mahatma and was acknowledged as India's leader by all except the majority of Muslims and some Christians. It was during my second year at St Stephen's that three revolutionaries, Bhagat Singh, Raj Guru and Sukhdev were hanged. All over India, schools and colleges closed as a mark of protest against the executions. Not St Stephen's. After the morning assembly another boy and I raised the slogan 'Bhagat Singh, zindabad!' We hoisted the Indian tricolour on the college flagmast meant for the insignia of St Stephen's; bearing a red cross and the college motto, Ad Dei Gloriam—to the glory of God. We were summoned by the acting Principal, an Englishman named Monk, to his office. He reprimanded us and warned us that if we did that sort of thing again we would be expelled from the College. I promised to behave myself and begged Monk not to report me to my father.

An incident that rankled in my mind for many years

occurred while I was holidaying in Shimla with my uncle and aunt. He was a member of the Punjab Legislative Assembly and very eager to be made a minister or a deputy minister. He was always calling on the Governor, Chief Minister and members of the Punjab Cabinet to plead his case. He was undoubtedly the ablest Sikh politician of his time, but he could not get ahead because, despite being a big landowner, he was not recognized as a Jat agriculturalist. At the time Punjab's politics was Jat-oriented. The only non-Jat minister was a Hindu; the Sikh minister was Sir Sunder Singh Majithia—a Jat with aristocratic pretensions. My uncle threw a large tea party at Davico's at its newly acquired premises above a cinema house between the Mall and Lakkar Bazar. Over three to four hundred of the elite of Shimla society, including ministers of the Punjab government, were present. I was then an avid collector of autographs and had in my album the signatures of Jawaharlal Nehru and Sarojini Naidu, among others. I could not get the signature of Bhagat Singh, so I simply stuck a photograph of the young man in one of the pages. I went round the tea party asking celebrities for their signatures. They did so without comment. Last of all I approached Sir Sunder Singh Majithia. He began to turn over the pages of my album to see whose signatures I had and came upon the photograph of Bhagat Singh. 'Why have you got this fellow's picture here?' he demanded angrily. 'Because he is my hero,' I replied without flinching. 'Hero!' scoffed the knight. 'He is a renegade.' (Bhagat Singh, a Sikh, had cut off his long hair and shaved his beard.) 'I will not put my name in an album with the picture of a renegade,' he shouted. Then he flung my album across the hall. I was shaken and broke down. Sewa Singh and his wife, who were close friends of my father, shouted back at Majithia: 'How dare you treat this boy in this way? He has every right to admire Bhagat Singh. We all do.' Majithia stormed out of the room. The party was a fiasco. My uncle and aunt were understandably upset. I was never able to forgive Sir Sunder Singh Majithia for his boorish behaviour—nor even respond to gestures of friendship made by his sons and grandsons,

As for Muslims, except for one boy who wore a Gandhi cap and dressed in khadi, the others sported red fez caps and wore distinctly Muslim dress. They did not speak the language of nationalism. On the staff was a history professor, Dr Ishtiaq Hussain Qureshi, who constantly harped on his Islamic heritage and supported separate electorates for Muslims. He was among the first to migrate to Pakistan and later became its education minister. This feeling of separateness on the part of the Muslims saddened me. I did my best to befriend them but had little success.

It is not quite accurate to say that I made no Muslim friends. A very happy and wholly unexpected bonus came through my sister, who was then studying in Lady Irwin College for women. She became friendly with a Muslim girl, Ghayoorunissa Hafeez from Hyderabad. She was invited for tea on Sundays. The first time she came she wore her burqa and had to be persuaded by my sister to take it off in our home. She was a frail, sallow-complexioned girl with curly, light-brown hair. Despite having been in purdah, she was quite saucy in her talk and behaviour with the boys she met in our home. I fell madly in love with her. I also realized that I had no hope of getting closer to her because of the distance that religion had created between us, and was quite happy just to know a Muslim girl I could call a friend. She was bolder than I. One evening, my sister and I took her to the pictures. She wore her burqa till the lights were dimmed. I sat between the two girls. As the film started, I felt her hand gently rest on mine. For a while I was not sure whether she was aware of where her hand had strayed or whether she had placed it there deliberately. To put my doubts at rest she pressed my hand gently and twined her fingers in mine. I was out of my wits with excitement and lost all interest in the film. In the interval, while my sister's attention was distracted elsewhere, I asked her whether I could write to her and take her out. She nodded her head. 'I have permission to go with your sister,' she said, 'you can come to fetch me and drop me back.'

Unknown to my sister, I began to pick up her friend every Sunday afternoon and take her out for long drives. At the time, my father had two cars: a new one which he drove himself and an old Fiat for the use of the family. This Fiat had a small lever close to the clutch which could be turned off to stop the flow of petrol into the carburettor. With my left hand I used to hold hers, while the right was on the steering wheel. She would not let me take any further liberties. One evening, I turned off the petrol lever in a secluded spot on the Ridge in the hope that I could draw her into my arms. She was familiar with such tricks and turned the lever on. 'If you don't behave, I will not see you again,' she warned me. I got no nearer Ghayoor than writing love letters to her from college in Lahore and in England. I was writing such letters to other girls as well.

More than thirty years later Ghayoor came back into my life and again through my sister, who was still unaware of what had gone on between us behind her back. By then Ghayoor had seen two husbands to their graves and was the mother of a lovely eighteen-year-old-girl, Fareesa, who was in the same college her mother had once attended, Lady Irwin. Ghayoor appointed me her local guardian. Fareesa turned out to be like her mother. On many occasions she left college on the pretext of visiting her local guardian but, instead of coming to my home, she went out partying. She had no problem extracting a letter from me to say that she had spent the day with us.

Ghayoor remained my friend into her eighties. Every time I went to Hyderabad I spent my spare time with her. It was Ghayoor's affection for me that made me an ardent lover of Muslims. For me, an Indian Muslim could do no wrong. I came to the conclusion that all you have to do is to fall in love with one person to love his or her community.

ENGLAND DAYS, AND
LOSING MY VIRGINITY

The sea voyage from Bombay to Southampton took eleven days, including a few hours' halt at Aden and Port Said. There was also a brief stopover at Ismailia to offload passengers who wished to visit the Pyramids and Cairo and rejoin the boat at Port Said. Quite often ships had to wait their turn at the entrance of the Suez Canal to take on pilots to steer them through the narrow seventy-mile long canal joining the Red Sea and the Mediterranean. It was slow going, with lines of ships in front and behind and a vast desert on either side, interspersed with nondescript, dusty habitations.

Most of the passengers in the economy class of the *Conte Rosso* were students from different parts of India.

There were over a hundred males and about a dozen women. The only one I knew well was Arjan Singh, who had been in my class at Government College. He had been to England the year before and was travelling first class with his father, Bawa Dinga Singh, a prosperous timber contractor. Arjan had told me of the great time he had had on his earlier visit, how easy it was to lay white girls and the preparatory exercise one could get for a small sum of money in the brothels of Port Said.

The only other face familiar to me was that of Som Nath Chib, who had been recently appointed a lecturer in Dayal Singh College, Lahore. A couple of weeks earlier he had married a well-known Lahore university beauty, Savitri Bhalla. For them it was a honeymoon voyage. They spent their time gazing into each others' eyes, kissing in front of everyone, then hurrying back to their cabin meant for two. Their amorous goings-on created much envy and gossip.

We were six males in one cabin. After the introductions were made, the gong sounded for lunch. Before going to the dining room, we went up to see the boat pull out of Bombay harbour and wave to our friends and relations who had come to bid us farewell. Then down the steps for our first repast on sea. No sooner had the soup been served than the ship began to heave and roll. It was monsoon time and the Arabian Sea was very turbulent. We left our soups unfinished and rushed down to our cabins. Some threw up in the washbasin; I managed to get on to my upper berth and overcome the nausea building up. I heard the ship groan and shudder as if it was about to break into pieces. For the next three days I left my bunk only to dash to the loo and back, to recover breath and equipoise. Occasionally the cabin steward brought me bread and fruit which I turned back. After three days and nights spent in agony, the *Conte Rosso* stopped rocking and rolling. We were out of turbulent waters. The next day the ship docked at Aden.

It was after spending some hours walking along Aden's bazars, largely owned by Indians, that I made the acquaintance of some of my fellow passengers. I will name only two who resurfaced in my life later. One was Lakshmi Kant Jha who made the I.C.S. and held many important positions in the government before he died at the age of seventy or so. He became Governor of the Reserve Bank of India, Ambassador to the United States, Governor of Jammu and Kashmir, and Chief Economic Adviser to Prime Minister Lal Bahadur Shastri. He also indulged in palmistry and horoscopy.

Though big and flabby, he ardently wooed young and beautiful women. Jha and I lived in the same pension in London for some months and continued to see each other in later years. There was also a certain Miss Nehru, a distant relation of the first prime minister of independent India. She always draped herself in handspun khadi and never missed an opportunity to sermonize us on how we should deport ourselves as 'ambassadors of India'. More about her later.

The voyage after Aden was sheer bliss. The Red Sea was placid as a lake. We played deck-tennis, quoits, table tennis or chatted with the girls. Warm winds blew over from the neighbouring deserts. At times migratory birds alighted on the ship; flying fish often landed on the deck. One evening, as the sun went down, the entire sea, as far as the eye could see, became alive with dolphins tumbling in and out of the water. At night the sky was brilliantly illuminated by a myriad stars. On moonlit nights the sea shimmered like a vast spread of quicksilver. Travelling by ship was so much more pleasurable than the non-stop flights I had to take later in life—getting drunk, over-eating hurriedly in cramped conditions, and watching films to kill the hours.

After offloading the party who wished to see the

Pyramids, we entered the Suez Canal. It was like being on a massive chariot gliding slowly through the desert, with the water barely visible from the middle of the deck. On the Egyptian side a road ran along the canal, past small villas and an occasional township: on the other it was a stretch of barren, uneven, dusty wasteland. It was during this part of the voyage that Bawa Arjan Singh enlisted the names of young men who wanted to lose their virginity at Port Said. I was not one of them.

We docked at Port Said for six hours. As soon as we disembarked, we were surrounded by greasy-looking men in red fez caps and jellabas trying to sell pornographic postcards and inviting us to savour the pleasures of Egyptian brothels! 'You no lublub?' they would ask, poking their index fingers into a hole made by the thumb and the index finger of the other hand. We shook them off, only to be accosted by others who pursued us till we got to our destination, Simon Artz's Department Store. I had not seen a store of that size; it was then the biggest in Asia. It was Jewish-owned but much the most frequented by affluent Egyptians. I simply looked around in awe without buying anything. Then I set out on the narrow causeway which led to the statue of Ferdinand de Lesseps, the architect of the Suez Canal. By the time I got back there was only an hour left for the *Conte Rosso* to depart. Before going up the gangway I was persuaded to buy a carton of dates— they were longer, darker and more luscious-looking than those I had seen in Hadali. I was able to beat the vendor to half the price and triumphantly went up to the deck to savour them. I discovered that beneath the top layer of a dozen dates there was only sawdust.

I warned fellow passengers who were buying things from boats tethered alongside the ship and having items sent up the baskets slung by ropes. Many bought boxes of chocolates only to discover there was nothing beneath the first layer; some bought perfumes with the names of French brands to discover the bottles contained scented oil. I have passed through Port Said and Cairo many times since then and have never bought anything in Egypt again.

That evening we heard of the adventures of the males who had visited the brothels. They had met no houris waiting to be deflowered by them: only middle-aged, fat Arab and Black women. Once inside the brothels, they had no escape. They were made to part with more money in tips than they had bargained for. This being their first contact with female flesh, they came as soon as they entered—some even spent themselves before making contact. What bothered them was the fear of having contracted venereal diseases because none of them had as much as seen a contraceptive. They spent the next two days examining their penises for tell-tale signs of syphilis or gonorrhea. Word of what the males had been up to got to the Nehru girl's ears. One morning she summoned us to a meeting. Without disclosing what she had heard, she reprimanded us for our disgraceful behaviour. 'Would you like your country to be judged by what some of you have been up to in Port Said?' she asked.

The Mediterranean remained blue and sunlit throughout our passage. We passed through the Straits of Gibraltar into the Bay of Biscay, notorious for its turbulence. We were lucky. So also with the English Channel which was equally well-known for its roughness. We docked at Southampton and took the boat-train to London. I had no address to go to.

Roma Biswas was on the platform of Victoria Station waiting to receive me. As I have already noted, my letters to her from Government College had been getting amorous. Once on vacation in Delhi I had gone to see her in Modern School. She had a suite of rooms on the roof. We sat and talked late into the evening. When we came out, the moon was full. Instead of saying goodbye to her, I grabbed her in my arms and violently kissed her on her lips. She remonstrated, 'Really, how can you?' I fled downstairs. Back in Lahore I wrote to her apologizing for my behaviour. She generously forgave me. But thereafter her letters had become as warm as mine. I was not sure how she would receive me.

I was not left in doubt. As soon as we got into the taxi which was to take us to the Indian Students' Union Hostel on Gower Street she put her arms around me and glued her lips to mine. We continued to kiss each other passionately till the cab pulled up outside the hostel. There was no room available. The secretary pointed to a pension across the road and asked us to try there. We went across with my valise. L.K. Jha was already there. The pension was run by an Italian named Serafino—a small, wizened man and his much larger English wife who did the cooking. I was shown into a small room on the top by one of the two maids serving in the establishment. The terms for bed and breakfast were within my means. I decided to settle there for the first few months. No sooner were we left alone than Roma and I fell on the bed, passionately kissing each other. I had not known a woman at close quarters and was unsure of what I should or should not do. I went on kissing her till her lips were sore. I struggled wildly to undo her sari. I could not hold myself. It was a messy business. I felt thoroughly ashamed and did not want to see any more of her.

'That is not love, that is lust,' she scolded me. But she had been roused and was unwilling to let me go. As I lay in bed feeling sorry for myself she came over to me. 'Promise you won't try this again!' she demanded. The mauling began all over again. And again it ended the same way. I felt nauseated with her and myself.

I did not want to take any more chances with Roma. It was time for dinner. We went and ate in a small wayside café. Mercifully, the rules of the pension did not allow women visitors after dark.

If Roma had been more experienced in dealing with teenagers, she might have become my mistress for the rest of her stay in England. What she succeeded in doing was to put me off her and off sex for many months. For the next few days she laid siege to the pension. I dodged every attempt she made to get me alone in my room. She gave up in disgust and went off with an older and more experienced student from Modern School. I lost track of her.

With London it was love at first sight. I fell in love with its streets, its beautifully done-up shop windows, its buses, tramcars, the Underground and its smells. Above all, its women and just about everything else. I spent the first few days getting to know it. I walked over to Tottenham Circus, down Oxford Street to Marble Arch, back to Oxford Circus and through Regent Street to Piccadilly Circus, Leicester and Trafalgar Squares. I sat on the steps of St Martin-in-the-Fields watching people feed pigeons; I listened to the chittering of millions of starlings. When the shades of twilight darkened I walked through the Strand to Holborn, Bloomsbury and back to the pension in time for supper.

In a few days life fell into a routine. The morning started with a lecture on Roman Law at University College. Our teacher was the very grim-faced, short-tempered Dr Jolowicz. Then I took a bus to King's College on the Strand. There the Dean of Studies, Dr Potter, lectured to us on English Law. Then across Aldwych to the London School of Economics to hear bi-weekly orations on politics by Professor Harold Laski, lectures on the Law of Tort by Professor Davies and on Constitutional Law by Professor Ivor Jennings. I walked back in the evenings through gas-lit Holborn, with the organ grinders grinding out popular tunes, past the British Museum and to the Serafino establishment. Often I had my dinner at the Indian Students' Hostel because it was the cheapest place for curry and rice. Once in a while I went to an Italian restaurant where you could eat a filling meal of pasta for under five shillings. During term time there were also dinners at the Inner Temple. One had to be dressed in black and wear a black gown. There were two bottles of port or red wine for every four diners. English students, ever thirsty for an extra glass, sought me out to make up their four so that they could take my share.

In November it turned cold. Then came pea-souper fogs: brown-and-yellow and pestilential. You could hardly see beyond your out-stretched hand. I caught a chill, followed by a cough and fever. The doctor I consulted advised me to get out of London for a few days. I took a train to some place in Buckinghamshire and found a room in a pub deep in the heart of New Forest. The fresh air and long walks amidst elm, oak and pine soon cleared my chest of colds and coughs. I felt on top of the world and was not eager to return to London.

One night after a longish after-dinner walk in the woods I reluctantly retired to my room on the first floor. I heard voices in the entrance hall asking for a room for the night. The female voice sounded familiar. I tiptoed out of the room and looked down the balcony. It was the sermonizing Nehru woman with a young Englishman. She had apparently spotted the name Singh in the guest register, but at that hour she had no choice and could not escape. The couple was given the room next to mine and spent the night together. Early next morning they left the pub without breakfast, which was included in the fare. When I went down to the dining room, I took a quick look at the register: they had put themselves down as Mr and Mrs English Something-or-the-other. A fitting epilogue to her sermons on how Indians abroad were ambassadors of their country and legends about the purity of Hindu womanhood! I ran into her at several Indian functions, like Gandhi's birthday and Diwali, and I was surprised that she had not rid herself of the habit of telling others how to behave in a foreign country.

There were times when I felt extremely lonely and homesick. I had got to know quite a few English students at college but they lived in distant parts of London. The Indians I met every evening at the Students' Union Hostel had their own groups and, apart from playing table-tennis with me, did not wish to add me to their friends. Jha was too occupied preparing for the I.C.S. and only came to my room to borrow my notes. Occasionally, the two English maids of the pension who came to do my bed tried to flirt with me. I did not have the guts to respond. They found Jha more responsive.

Across from my room was the University College Hospital. On Saturday nights they had dances for doctors, students and nurses. From my window I could see them whirling around. I caught the strains of Viennese waltzes and current favourites like 'Red sails in the sunset', 'Music goes round and round and comes up here' and 'Lambeth Walk'. Seeing other people happy and enjoying themselves made me more acutely conscious of my loneliness.

Weekends were the worst. After playing tennis or hockey at the college grounds at Mitcham I had nothing to do except make fair copies of my lecture notes or read law books. The bolder Indian men would go to Piccadilly Circus and pick up women to take to their digs. They told me that it was easy and cost them nothing more than giving the women a drink or two in a pub and some sandwiches at home. Then they played strip poker. The person who drew the lowest card had to discard a garment. Fifteen minutes of the game and both were as naked as the day they were born. Then they got down to business. I would hear those tantalizing stories, get worked up, but never acquired enough courage to follow their example. The best I could do was walk round the by-lanes of Piccadilly Circus, Shepherd's Market or Bayswater Road and ogle at prostitutes who frequented these areas. No one ever propositioned me. I got the feeling that if I approached them, they would snub me for no other reason than that I was dark and wore a turban and a beard.

On Sundays I went to Hyde Park. I would hire a boat and row up and down the Serpentine from end to end several times to burn out the excess energy which seemed to be centred on one point in my middle. It did not prove very efficacious. Strewn about the stretches of green lay couples in tight embrace, oblivious of passers-by. The English were too well-mannered to stare, but Orientals like myself could not keep our eyes off them. At times they lay one on top of the other with nothing more than a mackintosh or an overcoat over them. After a while such close proximity proved too much even for the cold-blooded English: their covering would start heaving rapidly and then collapse into a heap. If the copulation became too explicit, the police took the couple to a nearby station. They were let off after paying a small fine. The best I could do was re-create these scenes in letters to my cousin, Narinder. At times I would substitute myself in the letters for one of my friends at strip poker and tell him of the wonderful time I was having. The truth was that at the end of my first year in England I was still a virgin.

My one regret was that I had not been inside an English home. The one Englishman I knew well was C.H. Everett of the Indian Police who was doing a course in law at University College. He was a shy, reticent man. Nevertheless, he invited me to his wedding to the daughter of a retired I.C.S. officer who had been Commissioner of Karachi. After his honeymoon, Everett asked me to spend a weekend in the country home of his wife's parents. They were gracious but ill-at-ease having a coloured man as their house-guest. So was I. They dressed for dinner and followed the strict discipline of upper-class English families. The next morning they took me with them for the county fox hunt. Since I could not ride, I asked to be excused. But I did get to see the ritual of dress, the hierarchy observed among hunting types, the blowing of horns, the handling of beagles, a poor fox being run to death and having its tail (brush) cut off. Having achieved their object, glasses of sherry were passed round like prasad after a religious service.

Instead of spending my summer vacations in England I decided to return to India. I went to Genoa by train and once again took a Lloyd Trestino boat, the *Conte Verde*, for Bombay. This time I pretended to be an experienced traveller. On the way out, I had picked up a dozen Italian words and added a few more during my visits to Italian restaurants: buon giorno, buona sera, grazie, si, no, per favore, quanto costa? etc. Amongst the passengers were the Chibs returning home with their four-month-old daughter. They had got over the period of frenzied lovemaking. He was back at his books; she preoccupied with her child. We were placed at the same table.

Our next stop was Brindisi, which was twenty-four hours by sea from Genoa. Before we docked at Brindisi, Savitri Chib, who had noticed my speaking to the Italian waiters asked me, 'You speak some Italian, don't you?'

I nodded my head.

'Could you get me a packet of glycerine suppositories for a child? My daughter is constipated and I don't want to give her a laxative orally.'

I readily undertook to do so.

I did not have much trouble in finding a drug store. I scanned the shelves to see if I could spot glycerine suppositories. I couldn't. I decided to explain what I needed in my vocabulary of a dozen words. The pharmacist understood the word constipation and produced some brands of laxatives. I shook my head saying 'no, no'. Then pointed to my bottom with a crooked index finger. The pharmacist understood and produced an enema apparatus. I knew I was getting close to my quarry. Suddenly the Italian word for child came to me. I patted my belly (I should not have done so) and triumphantly shouted 'bambino, pore bambino'.

'Ah, si Signor!' exclaimed the pharmacist with an understanding look. And slapped a packet of contraceptives on the counter. I returned to the *Conte Verde* not with suppositories to relieve a child of constipation but with an anecdote to enliven many parties.

The rest of the voyage was uneventful. At Port Said it was another long walk to De Lessep's statue. I bought nothing. We did not stop at Aden, and the Arabian Sea was calm. Soon I was back in India. I spent the day wandering about Bombay and took the evening train to Delhi.

This time only members of my family came to receive me at the railway station. They were disappointed to see me as shabbily dressed as when I had left them. 'You must have come back from Aden,' my mother carped at me. It was the same when I went up to Shimla to spend a week with my uncle, aunt and their twin daughters. My uncle and aunt, who had been to the Round Table Conference in London some years earlier, had picked up a lot more in the few months they had spent there than I had in a year. He had a couple of Savile Row suits; she had learnt to speak English better, and cultivated a taste for English salads. Her favourite item was lettuce which she nevertheless pronounced as 'let oose'. My girl cousins, whom I accompanied on their evening walks, said that all I had learnt was Tarzan's cry when he summoned his monkey brigade by shouting 'yoo hoo'. However, I had an ardent listener in Narinder, whom I regaled with made-up stories of my seducing English girls.

The two months went by faster than I expected. Once more I took the Frontier Mail to Bombay to catch the *S.S. Victoria*—another Lloyd Trestino liner (we Indians avoided P & O boats as we had been told that English stewards did not show the same courtesy to Indian passengers that they did to the English). I arrived in Bombay in the afternoon. My ship was to sail next morning. I found a room for the night in the Victoria Terminus station where I had detrained. It was not a fortunate choice but, for reasons personal, a memorable one.

I left my luggage in my room and locked it. I went out to explore the neighbourhood. I found myself in a narrow lane with mean-looking shops below and women sitting by open windows on the floor above. As I looked

31

up, one of them smiled and beckoned to me. I ignored her solicitation and walked on. I discovered I was in the prostitute quarter, Kamatipura. I proceeded to the end of the lane and turned back. The woman who had beckoned me was still by her window. She again gestured to me to come up. 'Which way?' I asked her. She pointed to a staircase leading up to her room. I went up the dark flight of steps. There was a boy sitting there. The woman came to receive me. She was fat, dark, middle aged and dressed in a salwar kameez. Without a word of welcome, she said in Punjabi: 'It will be ten rupees.' I pulled out a ten-rupee note and handed it to her. She gave the boy a five-rupee note and ordered him to give it to her landlord. She bolted the door from inside.

It was a dark, dingy room lit by a single oil lamp. It had no furniture save her charpoy covered over with a greasy durrie and a dirty pillow. There was a pitcher of water with a lota covering its mouth. She turned round to address me. 'You Sardars are such fine-looking men, why do you grow this fungus round your chins?' she asked, running her hand over my beard. I did not reply. She sensed that I was a novice. 'Have you been to a woman before?' she asked.

'No,' I replied somewhat hoarsely. 'You are the first one.'

'You have nothing to worry,' she replied, 'I am quite clean.' She slipped off her salwar and tucked her shirt above her waist, baring her fat bottom. She went to the pitcher, filled the lota and splashed water between her thighs and dried her middle with a dirty rag. She laid herself on her back on the charpoy and raised her legs bent at the knees to her chest 'Come!' she said, stretching out both her arms towards me

Till then I had not so much as had a good look at a woman between her thighs. A fleeting glimpse of the hairy private parts of Kamala Bose, the Principal of the school I studied in, had revolted me. My vision of a woman's lower portion was what I had seen on marble statues, none of which had pubic hair. This dark, fat woman who lay before me with her knees touching her chin had shaved herself. I was not sure where to enter her. As I undid my trousers and bent over her, she took my penis in one hand and directed it to its target. As I entered her, I spent myself.

She was a kindly whore. She realized I had got very little for my money. 'If you want to do it again, it will cost you only five rupees,' she said, sitting up on her charpoy. I wasn't sure how long it would be before I would want to repeat the performance and excused myself. 'Come whenever you want to, you have nothing to worry about me,' she assured me. 'I will give you a much better time. You can touch my breasts and kiss me as well.'

I returned to my room at Victoria Terminus. The vision of my brief encounter would not leave my mind. I decided to return to the whore to have a second and perhaps a more satistying go. I found the gates of the station shut. The Gurkha guard told me that if I went out, I would not be allowed in till the morning. Reluctantly I returned to my room and relieved myself of the tension that had built up. I was not sure if I could describe that all too brief act of sex as losing my virginity. However, during the return voyage to England, I spent many anxious moments examining my penis for syphilitic sores.

Before leaving for my vacation I had shifted from Serafino's pension to a boarding house kept by a Miss Whaley of Knolly's Road between Tulse Hill and Streatham in southwest London, not far from Crystal Palace. 'The three-storeyed pension was along a railway track over which trains passed every five minutes. It took me a couple of days to get used to them. The other residents of Miss Whaley's boarding house were an elderly Scotsman, Armstrong, who shared her bedroom, a middle-aged lady who looked after a laundry establishment, an aged Scots brother and sister, the Dunsmuirs, two nurses, Miss Badge Barkham and Miss Lillian Booth, and a young English chemist.

The lodging had been found for me by Shoran Singha, Secretary of the Indian Students' Hostel, who had his house at the Streatham end of the same road, where he lived with his French wife and her daughter. I used to go to the Singhas twice a week to have lessons in French from his step-daughter. Also twice a week, I went to a young English girl to learn ballroom dancing.

I occupied an attic room next to Madge Markham's. She was a plain-looking woman in her thirties. Her colleague Lillian Booth was somewhat younger, full-bosomed and more attractive. I felt my chances with the plain-looking Madge were better than with the better-looking Lillian. Madge had got us tickets for a play written by her brother, which was having a good run in a West End theatre. I made a few passes at her and one night even tiptoed to her room and, despite her protests, kissed her. I had written to her from India. She had responded to my letters.

When I returned to Knolly's Road, I was given a larger room on the first floor at a slightly higher rent. As boarding houses went, I was better off than most Indian students. The biggest advantage was that I was in an entirely English and Scots milieu. In the evenings we sat together in the sitting room exchanging gossip, ate our dinner together and often stepped out for an after-dinner stroll on Streatham Common. Although it took me almost an hour by bus and train to get to college, I found the change worthwhile. Also in the vicinity lived an English student in my class named Dennis Wisdom. His father was the headmaster of the local school. Dennis often invited me to his home for a meal. I became a member of the Wisdom family. I later kept in touch with the Wisdoms and attended Dennis's wedding when I was posted in India House. Dennis became a solicitor. He prospered, bought a Rolls Royce and a large house beside the Thames. His young sister Cynthia also kept in touch with me and sent her children to stay with us in Delhi.

Indians abroad tend to stick together. They join Indian clubs, regularly visit mosques, temples and gurdwaras and eat Indian food at home or in Indian restaurants. Very rarely do they mix with the English on the same terms as they do with their own countrymcn. This kind of island-ghetto existence feeds on stereotypes—the English are very reserved; they do not invite outsiders to their homes because they regard their homes as their castles; English women are frigid, etc. I discovered that none of this was true. In the years that followed, I made closer friends with English men and women than I did with Indians. I lived in dozens of English homes and shared their family problems. And I discovered to my delight that nothing was further from the truth than the canard that English women are frigid.

I stayed in the Whaley household for over a year. The two nurses moved out to digs of their own—two bed-sitters with their own kitchenettes. Lillian had sensed that I was more attracted to her than to Madge. The day before she left, I had told her of a very good continental film showing in a small cinema in Hampstead. 'Why don't you take me along?' she asked. We met as arranged at an underground station and proceeded to the cinema. When the lights went out, she took my hand in hers. After the picture was over, we went to the pub for a drink and a sandwich and then for a stroll on Hampstead Heath. As we passed Keats's cottage, I recited the opening verse of 'Ode to a Nightingale' to her.

She was impressed and rewarded me with a kiss on my hand. We walked arm in arm to Kenwood and found a secluded spot to get to know each other better. It was exhilarating for me to be so close to a pretty girl only slightly older than I and smelling of lavender and starch. For the next year or two I saw a lot of Lillian. We went out for walks to Hyde Park, Kew Gardens, etc. We went to see pictures and to restaurants. She took me to see *The Swan Lake*. It was the first ballet I had seen. I could make no sense out of it. She often asked me to her room, where we kissed the hours away late into the night. I never got beyond what I had with Roma Biswas! I still did not have the nerve to take liberties like fondling breasts and more, but I am sure that she expected me to. And she did not realize that I was still a virgin (though not technically) and would have been grateful if she had taught me a thing or two about sex. Slowly, we drifted apart—without any rancour but with a sense of disappointment. I don't know what became of her.

Someone told me that Satinder Singh, who had been in my class at Modern School, was somewhere in London to study medicine. I was eager to meet him as I had no other Indian friend in England. But I did not know where to find him. One day I was on my way to college by the underground, and as the train doors opened, in walked Satinder. What was more, he had been admitted to the medical faculty of King's College. For the next couple of years we were together most of the time. He was good at games and a good sport when it came to women. He was often short of money and usually borrowed it from me. We ate our lunches together in the college cafeteria and played table tennis in the common room.

An incident in which we were involved took place in the college common room. A well-dressed, middle-aged Englishman introduced himself as a member of the British Foreign Service due for a posting in India. We introduced him to other Indian students. Suddenly there was a rash of thefts—most of the victims being Indians. One afternoon I was playing table tennis and had left my coat on the ledge where Satinder and this Englishmen were sitting. When I finished and put on my coat I discovered that my wallet was missing. I thought Satinder had played a practical joke on me, but he denied having taken it. My suspicion then turned on the Englishman. I tried to find out more about him. I did not have to wait long. A few days later a detective from Scotland Yard came to our college to check on those who had lost money. He told me that the fellow had been arrested. He had a long record of thieving and picking pockets. Amongst his other victims was an eighteen-year-old English girl whose yearly scholarship money had been taken from her handbag the day she cashed her cheque. I was amongst the many students asked to appear before the Bow Street Magistrate to render evidence if required. That was my first experience of British justice. We sat in the gallery listening to other cases being disposed of. I was amazed to see that almost all the accused pleaded guilty and received sentences of fines or imprisonment. Then came the turn of our 'foreign service' imposter. He was in handcuffs. With him was his wife, a smartly dressed, attractive woman in her early thirties. The fellow pleaded not guilty. On the magistrate's asking him if he wished to cross-examine any of his accusers, he pointed to me. I was asked to come forward and take the oath to tell the truth. I narrated the incident in the common room. He did not ask me any questions. The magistrate roundly ticked him off for being a disgrace to society and robbing poor students. In view of his record, he sentenced him to four years in jail. It took less than ten minutes to dispose of the case.

Satinder was a lot bolder with women than I. Every Saturday, after our game of tennis or hockey, he was able to pick up a girl to take home. His prowess amazed me because he was a man of few words and could hardly converse with anyone on any topic. I found that out for myself when we were holidaying in Paris. We were in a pension close to the Pantheon. Amongst the other lodgers there was a tall, slender, full-bosomed and broad-hipped Afro-American girl, Marie Stokes. She was doing a course in French Literature in the institute where I was attending classes in elementary French. I had many more opportunities of being with her than Satinder had. Although assured that my advances would not be repelled, I was unable to make any. Satinder warned me, 'If you don't fuck the Marie woman in the next three days, I'll fuck her for you.' I knew he meant what he said and pleaded for more time.

Meanwhile, in order to help me get over my nervousness, he introduced me to French bordellos. He got a copy of what was known as *The Pink Book*, which had a list of Parisian whorehouses with their addresses. Most of them were in the area of Gare St Lazare. We went to one. We were welcomed by the Madame and escorted to a large drawing room with mirrors for walls. She told us what it would cost; pourboire (tips) were extra. She clapped her hands. A dozen girls trooped in, all stark naked. While they twirled their pubic hair as if they were moustaches, champagne was ordered for them. We paid for the champagne and the services to be rendered. We pointed to the girls we wanted and were taken by them to their separate rooms. The one I had washed her privates in a bidet and ordered me to do likewise. She asked me if I would like to come in her mouth. 'Non!' I replied firmly. As in the past, the act was over within a few seconds. I had to wait for Satinder for almost half an hour before he emerged from his tryst looking very pleased with himself, with his girl smilingly asking him to come again. He called me a chootia (cunt-born) and again threatened to take Marie off my hands.

I staved off Satinder by pretending that I had at last succeeded in seducing Marie. I had only got to kissing her thick, painted lips. She construed this as the beginning of a love affair to be consummated later. It never was. A few days later she left for the States. We continued to correspond with each other. More than thirty years later she came to see me at Rochester, where I had a teaching assignment. She had put on an enormous amount of weight: the tall, slender girl I had met in Paris was a mountain of flesh. I took her to my apartment. She had travelled by bus through the night to come to Rochester. While she was having a shower, she told me of her two marriages and of the lovers she had had. She came out of the shower rubbing her enormous torso and behind and continued talking to me. I fondled her breasts and kissed her. 'Honey, you don't want to bed me now; you didn't do so in Paris when I was really beddable.' I gave up the feeble attempt. Later she taunted me: 'You didn't push me too hard or I would have happily given in.'

I saw more of Marie in her house in Detroit where she gave a large party for my wife and me. Her blind mother asked me to sit in her lap. 'Marie has told me so much about you; now I want to see you with my hands.' She ran her fingers over my turban, beard and face as if reading Braille. 'Now I know exactly what you look like,' she said. Marie also visited our home in Delhi. My children, who were told by my wife that Papa's girlfriend of college days was coming for dinner, eagerly awaited her arrival. She brought them gifts. They could not believe that Marie could ever have had any boyfriends. Marie became the subject of one of my short stories, 'Black Jasmine'. It was more fantasy than fact.

I was back in the Whaley's pension in south London. One evening there was a terrible row between Armstrong and the launderette lady. They never had liked each other. Armstrong was very drunk and abusive towards her. All of us were drawn into the quarrel on the side of the lady. Even though Miss Whaley was Armstrong's mistress she was constrained to order him to leave. He swore that he would depart the next morning but cut Miss Whaley out of his will. 'Not a penny of my property will go to you,' he warned.

The next morning Armstrong was repentant. He apologized to all the inmates save the launderette lady. Miss Whaley was more than eager to forgive him and let him stay. The Dunsmuirs, who were on specially cheap rates, also decided to stay on. The others, being on the side of the launderette lady, decided to find accommodation elsewhere.

The only accommodation I could find immediately was a pension run for Indian students by a widow and her son on Worseley Road, between Hampstead and Belsize Park. It was a wretched little place with four other Indian students, two Sindhis, a Bengali Muslim and a handsome young fellow from the Kumaon hills. We only met at breakfast and dinner. The sole advantage of the place was its proximity to Hampstead Heath, which I got to know, as they say, like the back of my hand.

I was not happy to be in entirely Indian company. That was not what I had come to England for. In the few months that I was in this pension, two events took place: one had a decisive effect on my future, the other was a trivial incident which I later converted into a short story.

First the trivial. The young man from Kumaon, I think his name was Shah, did not care to mix with us. After a few weeks he thawed towards me and began to open up. He had an English girlfriend—'from a very decent, upper-class family', he assured me many times. 'Not like the cheap waitresses and nurses most Indian men go out with. Very reserved, very dignified,' he said. After a few days I asked him how far he had got with her. 'I have told you, she's not that kind of girl,' he replied, somewhat irritated. 'She will never allow anyone to take liberties with her unless she really loves him.' Some days later he admitted that she had kissed him when he left and was probably in love with him. He was very pleased with the progress he was making. 'When will you do it?' I asked him. He didn't like my using such language. But that was evidently very much on his mind. One Sunday, he wore his best dark suit and liberally doused himself with cologne. He told me that the girl's parents were out for the weekend and he would be alone with her. I wished him luck.

He was back within an hour. I went to his room. He was lying on his bed looking very woebegone. I asked him what had happened. Had she refused to let him do it? 'Kucch na poochho Sardarji [don't ask me anything] hamara to dil toot gaya [my heart is broken].' The story as it unfolded was that, far from being unwilling, the girl had promptly taken Shah to her bedroom and undressed herself. She ordered Shah to do likewise. He dutifully divested himself of his clothes. They embraced. She took his uncircumcised penis lovingly in her hands and remarked, 'I see you are not a Muslim.' All the ardour drained out of the devout Hindu Brahmin from the Kumaon hills. He went limp. I used this incident in my story 'The Great Difference'.

The other thing that happened was the visit of the Maliks to England. They had brought their second son, Shubhchintun, who was very slow in his studies, to join an agricultural college in Kent. They also wanted to explore the possibility of finding a match for their daughter, Kaval. They were orthodox Sikhs; their future son-in-law had to be a Sikh. One Tarlok Singh had got into the I.C.S. that year. If they could get him nothing would be better. Failing him, they meant to look for other suitable Sikh boys studying in British universities. I was one of them. The families were known to each other, but the Maliks knew very little about me as a person. They rang me up. I invited them to tea in my digs. They arrived a little before time and were shown to my room. Mrs Malik took a good look around. She sat on my bed and lifted the pillow. She found a gutka

46

(a Sikh's daily prayerbook) under it. She made up her mind. If it could not be Tarlok Singh, I was the second best available. Being a senior engineer, Mr Malik was reluctant to give his daughter to the son of a building contractor who often sought his favours. But his wife's opinion always mattered more to him than his own. Besides, my father was by then a leading contractor, with a large chunk of real estate in the heart of New Delhi. Finally it was the small prayerbook under the pillow which proved to be my trump card.

Later that summer I ran into them again. I was holidaying at Windermere in the Lake District; they were in a fancy hotel at the lake's northern end at Bow Ness. One morning I rowed up to Bow Ness to have breakfast with them. They were impressed by my physical prowess. Mr Malik spoke to the lady who ran the hotel and I was offered a very reasonable rate should I spend the rest of my vacation there. The next day I shifted from my pension in Windermere to this hotel with a bar, ballroom and garden overlooking the lake. I hired a rowboat for a month and spent most of the time rowing, fishing for perch or walking in the woods in the surrounding hills. This was Wordsworth's country. I spent more time reading his poems than on my law books.

I thought I had got over my phobia of ghosts. One moonlit night when I was out walking in the woods I came across a small monument with a marble tablet. I was able to read the inscription. It marked the spot where some people had been struck by lightning and killed. I became nervous and felt the presence of the dead around me. I made my way back to the hotel constantly looking behind to make sure that I was not being followed.

Back in London. I did not return to Hampstead. While playing hockey I had made friends with a tall, handsome, golden-haired boy named Richard Reiss, who was studying engineering. He invited me to spend a Sunday with his family in Welwyn Garden City. I fell in love with the Reiss family. The father, Captain Reiss, had spent some time in India and was one of the founders of Garden City. Mrs Reiss was very much like Whistler's portrait of his mother—tall, grey-haired and dignified. She was a Quaker and a pacifist. There were Richard's sisters, all stunningly good-looking, fair and golden-haired like their brother. Their home was on top of a rise overlooking a golf course. On one side stretched a woodland of bracken, oak and cedar, and wild rhododendrons in full bloom. Why, I asked myself, did I have to live in London and not in this blissfully beautiful woodland township?

Mrs Reiss found me an ideal lodging. Professor F.S. Marvin, then in his late seventies, lived in a lovely double-storeyed cottage with a sizeable garden. He had an Anglo-Indian woman, Mrs Cremona, and her twenty-year-old daughter Doris to look after him. He had a spare room and was happy to have me as a boarder. His two sons lived away. I moved bag and baggage to Welwyn Garden City. It was the happiest period of my five-year stay in England.

I made many English friends. For one, there were people with whom I travelled every day to London and back. I joined the Deleon Tennis Club, and being reasonably good at the game played for it against other local clubs. Nearer Christmas, I found myself in a group of carol singers who practised singing with flute accompaniment on the morning journey to King's Cross. Amongst them was a young, dark-haired girl; Barbara Purdom, who was training to be a ballet dancer. Her father was a writer of sorts; her brother, a film actor. They were Roman Catholics. For reasons beyond my comprehension, Barbara took a fancy to me and in her juvenile enthusiasm determined to marry me. She often invited me over to her house to watch her practise her steps; she slipped love letters in my pocket in the train where she made it a point to sit next to me. I was more embarrassed than flattered by her attentions.

Among other friends I made was Jack Peel and his very pretty Estonian wife, who worked as a waitress in a cafe where I often dropped in for coffee on Sunday mornings. Jack was a born linguist, as fluent in German and Russian as he was in his native English. He was also an accomplished pianist and gave concerts in the village hall. He played tennis for a rival club. Sikhs were no strangers to him, for he had earlier befriended one Gurdial Singh who had walked away with his girlfriend. Through his command of foreign languages, Jack rose to be a senior executive in Lever Brothers and was put in charge of its East European division. He also acted as an interpreter for Winston Churchill in his meetings with Stalin at Yalta. When Jack's Estonian wife died, he married an equally attractive German girl, Erika, who bore him a son, Nicky. Through Jack I made many other friends in Welwyn, including the Ortons who lived in a small village, Weston, and the Behrmans, a German Jew turned a Christian English gentleman. I never lost contact with the Reisses or the Peels. Richard's daughter married a Haryanvi Jat, Randhir

Singh, who settled in the United States. When he came to see me, I treated him like a son-in-law. Jack and I continued to play squash at lunchtime when I was posted in the Indian High Commission in London. He and his wife have spent a few days with us in Delhi and whenever I'm in London we get together for a meal.

Apart from Paris, I didn't get to see much of Europe. While I was a student, I had spent a summer on the Cote d'Azur. An opportunity to visit Germany came shortly before the Berlin Olympics. The Germans were eager to see Indian-style hockey before they took on the Indian Olympic side. They invented a Joint English Universities Indian Hockey team to participate in a tournament at Weisbaden. Two students from Kings, both Sikhs, Basant Singh from Kenya and I, were included to give the side an authentic Indian look. Both of us were indifferent players.

In Germany I had my first exposure to anti-semitism. Around the playground were benches for spectators. A few of them were painted yellow with the word 'Juden' written on them. I understood what it meant. And while watching the preliminary trials I decided to sit on them rather than on the other benches. One of my hosts told me that the benches were meant for Jews. I replied that I knew, but meant to sit on them as I was a communist (which was not true) and anti-fascist (which I was). They were very upset. Instead of ordering me back to England, as the Captain of our side wanted to, they tried to get round me. I became the most sought after member of the side. I was invited to receptions only meant for Aryans. At one of them I met a huge, over six-feet-tall blonde, a full-bosomed German girl, the very prototype of an Aryan maiden of Hitler's dreams. Through an interpreter I told her that I had never seen as handsome a woman as her in my life. I am not sure how my compliment was conveyed to her in German, but later that evening she came to my room in the hotel and told me in broken English that, since I had liked her so much, she was there to give me a good time. I might have accepted her offer but for one sentence she used: 'Why do you like Jews so much?' That put me off because, in fact, I had liked the few Jewish people I knew at King's more than others. There was Bronowski, who had changed his name to Baron. He played table tennis for England and ended up as Chief Justice in some African country. There was Lewinsohn, who helped me prepare for my exams. He became a prosperous solicitor. And there was a Miss Jaffe, the brightest girl in our class. She had a nervous breakdown while taking her final exam and was unable to do all the papers. Nevertheless, the examiners gave her a first division. I go out of my way to befriend Jews.

The four selected German teams did not have much trouble beating our quickly assembled rag-tag side of Indian college boys. But they did not learn much technique from us. When it came to playing against our Olympic Eleven the German side collapsed like a pack of Jokers.

When I returned to Welwyn, I found that quite a few men and women I had known in Delhi had arrived in England. First and foremost there was Kaval Malik who had come to do a course in the Montessori system of teaching. She had blossomed into a ravishing beauty, and she knew it. She often mentioned that her vital statistics were exactly those of a succession of girls crowned Miss Universe. Pratap Lal, with whom I had exchanged turbans at school to symbolize a fraternal relationship, came to do law and journalism. The two were in the same pension run by the Bell family in Ealing. E.N. Mangat Rai, who got into the I.C.S., came to do his probation at Keble College, Oxford; and Amarjeet Singh, who had been admitted to some college in Cambridge, came to do his tripos.

Both Pratap and Amarjeet were very keen on Kaval. Amarjeet, being a Sikh and already having a sister married to Kaval's eldest brother, rated his chances high. Pratap had the advantage of seeing more of her. Mangat Rai was then indifferent and even somewhat hostile to her. I saw quite a bit of these people. Once Mangat Rai, Richard Reiss and I went cycling through Oxford and the Cotswolds. Another time Pratap Lal and I cycled to Tintern Abbey and Wales. At Tintern, much to my chagrin and Pratap's delight, the lodge keeper took me to be his father. However, his seven-year-old daughter had seen through my beard and pronounced us to be of the same age. Once Amarjeet came to stay with me in Welwyn. He made a great hit with Professor Marvin because he could play a few bars of Chopin on the piano. One afternoon while strolling in the woods he was accosted by an elderly lady who asked him questions he could not answer. 'I am not the Singh you know,' he told her. 'I am a friend of his staying with him.' The lady apologized, 'I knew you looked somewhat different,' she said. An hour later when Amarjeet was waiting to catch his train to Cambridge, the same lady came to him and said, 'Mr Singh, you know I mistook a friend of yours for you.'

My chance to win over Kaval Malik came the following Christmas. I had spent the previous Christmas at a Quaker Hostel in Seer Green Halt not far from

Beaconsfield, Milton's cottage where the poet had written *Paradise Lost*, and Stoke Poges Churchyard where Grey had composed his famous *Elegy*. I asked her what her plans were for Christmas. She had none. And the Bells were planning to take a holiday and close their establishment for a few days. I suggested she come along with me to the Quaker Hostel. It was a quiet place largely frequented by elderly widows. I told her of the Friends Meeting House, the Mayflower barn in which we could play badminton and table-tennis, the graveyard where the Perm Brothers went buried and the woods surrounding the place.

The hostel was run by a widow, Mrs Cuthbertson. I told her what fun I had had the year before. She replied that she would have to seek her parents' permission before she said yes. She wrote to them. I was pleasantly surprised to hear they agreed to let her go with me. So a few days before Christmas we took a slow train to Seer Green Halt in Buckinghamshire. An old lady who plied the only taxi from the station to the village dropped us at the Quaker Hostel.

I laid siege to Kaval Malik's heart. During the long walks we took to visit Milton's cottage and Stoke Poges churchyard I tried to impress her with my knowledge of English poetry. I did not know much Milton but had refreshed my memory of the elegy. When we got there I recited the first verse; she did not know it and was suitably impressed when I told her it had been composed where we stood. 'And listen to this,' I continued:

> Full many a gem of purest ray serene.
> Dark unfathomed caves of ocean bear,
> Full many a flower is born to blush unseen,
> And waste its sweetness in the desert air.

I could sense that I had made my mark. None of her other friends had courted her in verse. Although she shrank back if I tried to touch her, her defences began to crumble. While we were at the Quaker Hostel she received several long letters from Pratap Lal. They were full of snide remarks about me and how unpleasant it must be for her to be in the company of a hairy Sikh. He was a gifted writer and a cartoonist. She showed me his letters. I had further confirmation that he was out of the running.

On the way back to London I proposed to her. She accepted my proposal, subject to her parents' approval. I wrote to my father telling him of what had transpired and asked him to call on the Maliks. He did. They expressed consent. We announced our engagement. Pratap Lal accepted it in good grace and we remained good friends. Many years later we stayed with him in

Bangalore where he was General Manager of Hindustan Aeronautics and saw a lot of him when he became Air Chief Marshal and Chief of the Indian Air Force. He died in London in 1978. Amarjeet, who had crossed my path many times and never liked me made the acid comment: 'His father's bank balance won.'

Another young man who had given his heart to Kaval Malik was Bharat Ram, scion of one of India's richest families. He was by then married and the father of a son. However, he kept in touch with her for many years till he realized that he could not put me out of the scene. Bharat's family, including his father Sir Shri Ram, came for a holiday to Europe. A few days later Kaval accompanied them to a spa in Germany. I betook myself to the French Alps for a skiing holiday.

Having won her over I was beset with doubts as to whether I had done the right thing. The one person who kept telling me that I had made a mistake was Mangat Rai. He had a poor opinion of Kaval's mental capabilities and did not even rate her looks very high.

Our correspondence began to drag. She found my enthusiasm for skiing and the snows very tiresome. In one picture postcard she sent me from Nuremberg she wrote of a great rally she had witnessed and of 'a new German leader, somebody called Adolf Hitler'. This was at a time when everyone in Europe was talking of nothing else except Hitler and the menace of Nazism. Evidently she didn't read newspapers or books, besides those prescribed in her curriculum. By the time she left for India with the Shri Ram family our ardour for each other had cooled considerably. Besides, I had begun to have doubts about my own future.

For the heck of it, I decided to have a go at the I.C.S. examination. I had only one chance; I knew that my academic record was loaded against me. I did the best I could. I believed my top-scoring subject would be International Law. I skipped one paper because I thought I would fare badly in it. Came the viva voce, I went to it as badly dressed as I always was, in an ill-fitting dark suit, a red tie and a blue turban. The first question the panel of three members asked me was why I wanted to get into the I.C.S. I replied candidly that I knew I had little chance of making it, but since it was regarded as a test of intelligence I thought I would have a go at it. They laughed. Other Indian candidates had replied to the same question by saying they wanted to serve the people, serve the country, etc. Next they asked me whether while studying law, I had ever visited the courts in England and seen how justice was administered. I told them of my having appeared as a witness before the Bow Street Magistrate and of my surprise at how speedily the case had been disposed of, the number of accused who had pleaded guilty and the severe sentences passed for petty thefts. And how hard English Barristers must find it to make a living. They had another hearty laugh.

The results were announced a month later. I had missed the I.C.S. by one place. Contrary to my expectations, the examiner had given me low marks in International Law. If he had given me another eleven, or if I had scored the same in the paper I did not take, I would have made it. And that for the single reason that I was the only candidate, Indian or English, who was given full marks in the viva voce: 300 out of 300. I was also recommended for nomination as a member of a minority community. They took a Muslim, a Christian or a Sikh by rotation every three years. Mohan Singh, who was then a Member of the Secretary of State's Advisory Council for India, rang me up to congratulate me and sent a telegram of congratulations to my father. For a week I rode on cloud nine, decided not to bother with my law exams and dreamt of another year in England doing my probation in Oxford or Cambridge. And to then return home triumphantly as a member of 'God's own service'. Unfortunately for me, a Sikh had been nominated a year earlier and a Christian a year before that. The nomination thus went to a Muslim. I was desolate. Come to think of it, I might have ended my career as a Secretary to the Government instead of struggling for years with law, journalism and writing books.

While on my skiing holiday, I heard that I had done poorly in my L.L.B. examinations. I had just managed to pass but would have to take one paper again. I had scraped through my bar examination and rejoined college to take a Masters degree in Law. My tutor, Dr Potter, told me bluntly that I was not up to it. After six months of struggling with the L.L.M. course I gave up the battle and decided to return home. I would have had to spend another six months to get my Barrister's certificate but a letter prompted by Kaval's father and from Sir Maurice Gwyer, the retired Chief Justice of India and then Vice-Chancellor of Delhi University, helped me to get the licence in absentia.

My days with Professor Marvin came to an abrupt end entirely because of me. We had got on very well with each other. He let me drive his car. I helped him in keeping his garden tidy, mowed and swept his lawn and chopped firewood for the winter months. One afternoon an English girl dropped in to see me. She was impressed that I was boarding with as distinguished a man as Marvin, who had written many books. 'Come and meet him,' I said, taking her by the hand. We burst into Marvin's study. He was deep in his thoughts facing his typewriter and visibly upset at being disturbed. I cheerfully introduced the girl and started telling him who she was. He went pale with anger and exploded, 'Don't you see I'm busy? Get out both of you!' I was badly shaken by his outburst. I took the girl home through the woods. I couldn't forgive Marvin for his rudeness. For the next few days I avoided talking to him. This time he was upset and had to explain why he had lost his temper. I had no forgiveness in me. I moved out to a boarding house in Welwyn Garden. Then at Peel's suggestion I went to live with his friends Maurice and Brenda Orton in Weston village some miles away from Letchworth Garden City. Since I had finished with college and was only working on one paper for the Bar finals I had plenty of time on my hands. I found the End Cottage very convenient. The Ortons worked in London. They left in the morning and returned late in the evening in time for supper. I had their cottage all to myself.

The Ortons were an odd couple, of a kind I had never met before. He was a tall, blond, powerfully built man from a working-class family with very little education. He was able to conceal his lack of education by adopting an upper-class accent. She was a petite, dark-haired, sophisticated Jewish girl who had been to university. They had met at a party where Maurice had read some of his poems and created the impression of being a working-class poet of the future. They had got talking over drinks that followed the poetry reading session. She had gushed with admiration. He simply took her by the hand to the host's bedroom and proceeded to fuck her. Brenda had never experienced such down-to-earth copulation, devoid of any preliminaries. A few weeks later they were married.

It did not take long for Brenda to find out that Maurice was a boor, prone to violence, and wanted a new woman every few days. He could not hold any job for long and blamed the bourgeois society in which he lived for not recognizing his genius. When out of a job he took it out on Brenda. When I moved into their cottage he had set his sights on a nineteen-year-old village girl called Fiona. He insisted on Brenda inviting her home. When he went to drop her back, he tried to take liberties with her. Her mother saw them and told Brenda about it. Another time he picked on an Indian girl and invited her to spend the weekend with them at

Weston. He tried to molest her. She was thoroughly frightened and refused to leave my side till she left. There were days when he got into a cussed mood and refused to let Brenda leave for her office. He abused her—'bitch! whore!' and threatened to beat her if she stepped out of the cottage. Brenda was reduced to tears but was too scared to disobey him. One weekend he came to Paris with me and insisted I find him a woman to sleep with. 'Go and find one for yourself,' I told him. 'I don't want any whore. I want one of your girl friends. They'll never forget me after they've had this,' he said, opening his fly buttons and yanking his penis out. It was the biggest penis I had ever seen—almost the size of a donkey's. We returned to Weston with him grumbling about having wasted his time and money. I felt very sorry for Brenda but could do very little to comfort her. Despite Maurice, I spent a happy two months in the End Cottage, going on long walks in the morning and riding in the afternoons. But I was finally happy to get away from the Ortons. Later, I heard from Jack Peel that Maurice joined the Air Force and was killed in an air crash in the early months of World War II. A very relieved Brenda took a second husband and was editing a women's journal.

I returned home somewhat shamefacedly. Gossip had gone round that my engagement was at breaking point. I had taken five years to pass exams others had done in three. When my father's friends came to congratulate him on the return of his son and asked him, 'Kaka kee paas kar ke aya hai?'—What has your son passed? he would reply, 'Hor tey pata nahi time bahut paas kar ke aya hai'—I don't really know what he has passed except that he has passed a lot of time. When told that her grand-daughter was to marry a Barrister, Kaval's grandmother remarked, 'Hai! Hai! Itt putto tay Balister nikalda hai'—You pull up a brick and you'll find a Barrister under it.

The one person who was genuinely glad to see me back at home was my grandmother. She celebrated my homecoming by getting her cronies together and, with the slapping of a drum, sang village ballads about the return of warriors. The strain proved too much for her. The next morning she went down with a mild fever. It did not deter her from having her early morning bath, spinning her charkha all day while muttering the 'Psalm of Peace' and feeding the sparrows in the afternoon. They came by the hundreds to pick up the morsels of stale chapattis she tore into tiny bits to fling at them. The fever got worse. But she refused to give up her

ENGLAND DAYS, AND LOSING MY VIRGINITY

daily routine of prayer, spinning and feeding sparrows.
One morning she was unable to get up. Doctors were
summoned. She knew her end was near. She sent for
the family accountant and asked him to take down
what she wished to be done with the little cash and
jewellery she owned. An hour later, with her two sons
and grandchildren around her sickbed, she bade us
farewell and passed away.

Her body was laid out on the floor of the veranda
where she used to spend most of the day spinning and
feeding sparrows. They flocked there as they used to
every afternoon. My mother threw them bread-crumbs.
Either because of the coming and going of mourners, or
the wailing and the keertan organized before her body
was taken to be cremated, the crumbs remained
unpicked. My grandmother became the subject of a
profile I wrote many years later when I was posted in
Ottawa and published in *The Canadian Forum* under the
title 'Portrait of a Lady'. It has remained my most
popular story.

The most awkward was my meeting with Kaval. The
silence between us had been construed as a break up of
our past commitments—rejection of the other by both.
We talked about it for over an hour, felt that if we
called off the engagement it would bring a bad name on

our families and, since there was no real reason to break up, we decided to go ahead with our plans to get married. I was for delaying it by a few months till I had found a place in Lahore where I intended to set up legal practice. My father had forestalled the problem and rented a two-bedroom corner flat in a newly constructed building on the main highway of the city, The Mall, facing the High Court.

The three months between my return home and my marriage I spent in the chambers of Kirpa Narain, who handled my father's legal business and was one of Delhi's leading lawyers. I took little interest in the briefs he asked me to prepare. I spent more time in Sessions Courts listening to murder cases than those concerning disputes over property. The evenings I spent with Kaval—doing the rounds of Delhi, going to the pictures with the Bharat Rams or for a swim in their pool.

Our marriage was an elaborate affair. Kaval's father was the first Indian Chief Engineer of the C.P.W.D. and this was his only daughter's wedding. My father was by then the leading building contractor and the largest single owner of real estate in the capital. He had been giving presents to other people's children for many years. It was his turn to receive them through his second son.

It was a traditional Sikh wedding, with a brass band leading the procession and me, draped in a bridegroom's veil of jasmine flowers, riding sword in hand on a white horse. The Maliks lived on 1 Tughlak Road, which was a bare furlong down the road from my father's house, 1A Janpath. We went through the ritual of being received by the bride's relations and my being put through a lot of banter and practical jokes by her cousins, followed by a feast. I spent the night in the Malik home. Early next morning, under a vast canopy we sat in front of the Granth Sahib, she demurely covering her face behind a veil; I in a cream coloured sherwani and chooridars with a gilded kirpan in my hand. The Anand Karaj (ceremony of bliss) was a solemn affair with ragis singing wedding hymnals. I couldn't resist the temptation of slipping my hand under her dupatta, in which she was covered, and tweaking her feet. We went round the Granth Sahib four times, I in front, she following me holding one end of a scarf which I had in my hands. We took our marriage vows—to remain faithful to each other and look upon others as our brothers and sisters. This was on the morning of 30 October 1939.

The same evening my father arranged cocktails and a dance party on the spacious lawn in front of his house. Over 1,000 people responded. Scotch, champagne, wines and brandy flowed; ballroom dancing on a specially laid out wooden floor went on till the early hours. Among the guests was Mr M.A. Jinnah who lived across the road and occasionally dropped in to inspect my father's rose garden. We were allowed to retire at midnight to consummate our marriage. I was later told that one of the drunken guests had run his car over a telegraph peon on his way to deliver a congratulatory telegram. The news was suppressed.

The wedding night is something every bridal couple looks forward to. I did my best to follow the traditional pattern. It was then that I discovered that my bride was a virgin. We had never talked of sex till then nor had she allowed my hands to go exploring beneath her waist. She pleaded with me to be patient. I gave in.

The next evening we left for Mount Abu for our honeymoon. It had been my choice for no other reason than that the entrance of Welwyn Garden City railway station displayed a large poster depicting a marble temple with the legend, 'Visit India: Dilwara temples at Mount Abu'. My English friends asked me if I had seen the place. I admitted I had not but would do so as soon as I returned home. We had to break journey at Ajmer where we were guests of Uttam Singh, an executive engineer working under my father-in-law and his remarkably young and pretty Hungarian-Jewish wife Maidy. No one could understand why she had married a grey-bearded Sikh older than her father. She had come to India with her mother, who matched Uttam Singh in age more than her daughter did. Maidy proved to be a devoted and faithful wife. It was only after her husband died that she consorted with John Martin, Headmaster of Doon School, and married him. A couple of years after Martin's death Maidy was murdered in her cottage in Dehradun. We spent the night at the Uttam Singh's. I could not make any progress with my bride.

The next morning we drove up to Mount Abu. A spacious bungalow of the C.P.W.D. overlooking the Nakki Lake had been reserved for us. Cook, bearer, ayah and gardener were at our disposal for a week. Also membership of the club and freedom to savour whatever it had in its cellars. We drank up all its stock of English cider. There was also a rowing boat to explore the Nakki. We spent the morning chasing a couple of otters till we drove them out of the lakes to the hills. The English Resident of the Rajputuna States threw a banquet for us where the local Sahib gentry and their ladies were present. Our stock in Mount Abu went up.

It was the first time that we had tasted Scotch and joined in drinking a champagne toast proposed to us. We returned to our bungalow somewhat light in our heads and feeling on top of the world.

The night was made for loving. A full moon shone on the Nakki and across our beds laid out in the airy veranda of the first floor. The gardener had strewn jasmine and rose petals on our pillows. This time nothing would hold back my ardour and she was mutely ready for what was to come. A little she protested before saying yes; I hurt her a little. A little she bled but our union was at last consummated.

We returned to Delhi still hungering for each other's bodies when I was ordered by my father to go to Mian Channu where Uncle Ujjal Singh was reported to be in poor health. I did as I was told and was away for an agonizingly long week. He was convalescing from his illness and permitted me to return to Delhi.

The honeymoon was over. I had now to set up home and a law practice in Lahore—both entirely dependent on my father's bounty. He gave me a brand new Ford in which to drive up to Lahore with my newly acquired wife, a flat to live in, and a chamber on Fane Road to receive my clients. My father-in-law furnished our flat. My father's closest friend, Basakha Singh, gave me all the law books I needed as a wedding present. Now it was for me to make a go of the legal profession. Or make a flop of it.

TO THE VICTOR GO
THE SPOILS

There are two themes I wish to illustrate through this almost entirely true short story. The first is that God compensates women He does not endow with good looks in His own mysterious ways. A plain-looking, homely type of girl need not envy her better-looking sisters because men are more likely to make passes at her than at girls who resemble Marilyn Monroe or Prema Narayan. He makes good-looking lasses haughty and arrogant and only gigolo types have the confidence to approach them. That is why the plainer-looking have a better time with men and end up making better marriages than pretty ones who seldom have a satisfying sex life and usually make disastrous marriages.

The second theme is somewhat hackneyed: only the brave deserve the fair, equally well expressed in the maxim, 'Nothing ventured, nothing gained.'

Now to the illustrative story.

Some thirty years ago I was living in a two-bedroom basement flat in Highgate, London. I had recently resigned from the diplomatic service but still had my large American limousine with a 'CD' numberplate and a sizeable stock of duty-free champagne, Scotch, wines and liquors. My family had returned to India and I had three months of freedom to finish a book I was working on and whatever else I wanted to do in the way of keeping myself amused. The apartment above mine was occupied by a stenotyping agency which closed in the evening. The one above the agency was occupied by a young lady who, I was told, was a stage actress. She went to work late in the evening and returned home after the second show, sometime after midnight. All three flats had one entrance. Since the only garage attached to the premises was too small to house my limousine, it was parked outside the entrance. The only source of natural light for my basement flat was a large window, half of which was above ground level alongside a bus stop. Sitting in my armchair I could see the legs of people queueing up outside or alighting from buses.

I spent most of the day working on my book. In the evenings, a girl who had been my secretary at India House came to collect whatever I had scribbled during the day and have tea with me before she departed. After she had gone I took a walk round Hampstead Heath and returned home to light a fire, drink, listen to music, eat a sandwich supper and read till I felt sleepy. This was rarely before midnight. And soon I began to time my retirement with the sound of the opening of the entrance door and the footsteps of the actress girl going up the stairs to her apartment.

It was a few days later that I discovered her identity. The lady who came to clean my flat also did the other two apartments. One morning I casually asked her about the occupant of the top flat. 'That be Miss Dawson,' she replied, 'Jennifer Dawson, pretty as a picture she is. And very very nice too. She gave me two free tickets for her show. She's got a very small role. But mark my words, she'll go far. One day I'll be proud of having worked for her.'

Thereafter I kept a lookout for the last bus which stopped by my apartment. And soon got to recognize the pair of shapely legs that alighted and then took their owner up the steps.

One Sunday morning I contrived to make her

acquaintance. I had noted that she went to the mid-morning service and since there was no show on Sundays, spent the afternoons at home, presumably washing her clothes. As soon as I heard her footsteps coming down, I came out of my apartment. She extended her hand and said, 'We are neighbours but we have never met. I am Jennifer Dawson. Mrs Markham has told me you are Mr Singh. Nice to meet you.'

I took her proffered hand and replied, 'Mrs Markham told me you were pretty but not how pretty you were. I am honoured living beneath a famous actress.'

'Famous my foot!' she said with a laugh. 'I am only a miserable extra. If you want to see how extra I am, I will be happy to give a ticket for the show. That's the only thing I can afford; I get it free.'

I opened the front door for her and asked, 'Can I drop you anywhere? I have nothing much to do except take my car for an airing.'

She looked at my chariot-sized limousine. 'Cor blimey! Must drink up gas by the gallon! I am going to the church round the corner, I don't mind being driven in your American Rolls Royce.'

I dropped her at the church. 'I can pick you up on my way back; how long will the service last?' I asked.

'You are most kind!' she replied. 'I should be through in an hour. Sure you don't mind?'

'On this fine Sabbath morning I have nothing whatsoever to do save eat the English air. Allah is in His heaven and all's right with the world.'

I went back to my apartment to freshen up and was back outside the church. I switched on the radio. I was lucky. It was Beethoven's Ninth Syinphony, the only piece of Western classical music I was familiar with. It was coming across in all its mellifluous beauty.

She was among the first to step out of the church. She shook hands with the vicar and ran towards the car. She certainly was a beauty: hazel-brown hair tumbling down on her shoulders, broad forehead, large brown eyes, lovely neck and as shapely a figure as you would see in a Miss Universe beauty contest. Beethoven's magic worked. 'Let's not go home till the symphony is over,' she pleaded.

I drove slowly round the heath, along Spaniard's Inn Road and the Vale of Heath. She kept humming softly to herself and tossing her head to the music, completely oblivious of my presence. We were passing Keats' Grove when the symphony reached its climactic end. 'That was wonderful,' she sighed. 'Thank you ever so much for indulging me. I have wasted all your precious morning.'

'It was a pleasure,' I replied. 'I wish you would waste

more of them. I get awfully lonely having no one to talk to except Mrs Markham and my secretary for a few minutes every day. The rest of the time, it is books. And silence.'

She did not rise to the bait. Nor accept my invitation to have a bite with me before she went up. 'Who will do all my laundry and ironing, write my weekly letter to Ma and cook my supper? Thanks for a wonderful time.' She patted me on the shoulder and ran upstairs.

Next Sunday I slipped a note under her door inviting her for a drink in the evening after she had done her Sunday chores. She did not send a reply but as it turned dark and the street lights came on, I heard her footsteps come down the stairs and a gentle tap on my door. I leapt up from my chair to welcome her. 'It is very thoughtful of you to have invited me,' she said. She looked round the dimly lit room with only one tablelamp above my armchair. I switched on the room light and went to help her take off her overcoat. 'It's freezing cold. Don't mind if I keep it on?' she asked.

Mrs Markham always laid coal in the grate. I took a bottle of gin and splashed it over the heap and threw a lighted match on it. The grate exploded into a blue flame and soon we had a blazing fire going. 'How extravagant can one be!' she exclaimed. 'Never heard of anyone lighting fire with gin.'

'Duty-free diplomatic privilege,' I replied. 'Costs me very little and is quicker than newspapers or woodchips to get fire going. What would you like, Scotch, sherry, gin, vodka, champagne?'

She slipped her overcoat off her shoulders and warmed her hands before the grate. 'If you are flush with liquor I would not mind some champagne,' she replied.

I got a bottle of Mouton Rothschild from the freezer, uncorked it with professional skill and poured the frothing, bubbling liquor into the best cut-glasses I had. I raised mine and proposed the toast, 'To the most beautiful girl in the world!' Her face flushed with pleasure as she raised her glass and replied, 'To the world's nicest old man and the greatest liar.'

She curled up in an armchair and sipped champagne; I replenished her glass several times. The fire in the grate glowed on her face and lit the curls on her hair. 'Jennifer, you must have lots of admirers and boyfriends,' I said.

'Why do you say that?' she asked.

'Now you are fishing. Your mirror must tell you why every time you look into it.'

'You are nice!' she replied. 'Believe it or not I have never had any boyfriends. Admirers, yes. A few. They pay me compliments. And that's that.'

I paid her more compliments. Quoted lines I knew of English peets in praise of beautiful women. She listened with a distant look in her eyes gazing into the embers of coal glowing in the grate. I put on music. She shut her eyes.

I made sandwiches and coffee and brought them in a tray for her. I gently tapped her on the shoulder. 'Asleep?'

She woke with a start. 'Not really. Day-dreaming to the music. I should have been doing all that, not you,' she said, looking at the tray. 'You are spoiling me.'

We ate our sandwiches and drank our coffee in silence. I felt her large eyes fixed, questioning, on me. Could I dare make an advance? No, she was too beautiful for the likes of me and I did not want to lose her friendship by taking a false step. After a while she stood up. 'I don't want to go but I must drag myself away. Beauty sleep and all that—can't afford to look dowdy on the stage.' She gave me a peck on my nose. 'Thank you for a wonderful, wonderful evening.' She left and shut the door behind her.

I had established rapport, proved that I was a gentleman who would not take unwelcome liberties with her. The rest, I would leave to time. And her. I changed my working hours to suit hers.

Every night she came back from the theatre, I had the fire lit, a bottle of champagne in the freezer, sandwiches on a tray and a steaming pot of hot coffee. She had her nightcap with me. We spent our Sundays together. She told me that she went to church because she had nothing better to do and much preferred to drive out to the country, walk in the woods and end the Sabbath by my fireside. We did Kenwood and Kew; Burnham Beeches and the Costswolds and Stratford-on-Avon. I got no closer to her than I had on the first evening.

Then an old friend of my college days in Lahore arrived in London. He had very little money and gratefully accepted my invitation to stay with me. He was a small, effeminate Sardarji whose chief qualification was being a good listener. No one would suspect him of a being a ladies' man or regard him as a rival. I told him about Jennifer, her goddess-like aloofness, and cautioned him to treat her with respect.

The first time they met he was on his best behaviour. She gave him a ticket for her show. They came back together. I was happy they had hit it off. The following Sunday I asked a few Indian friends we had known in Lahore and their wives for drinks. Needless to say, Jennifer was the main attraction. And a great success.

She acted the hostess and talked to all the women. From the way my guests looked at me I could sense that they felt Jennifer was my woman and I had something very nice going for me while my family was away. I did not want to disabuse them.

The party went on late in the night with vast quantities of Scotch and champagne going down their gullets. Everyone was in high spirits, particularly my house-guest who took more than his share of liquor. Around midnight, the guests departed, leaving Jennifer and the Sardarji with me. They relaxed in their armchairs while I removed empty glasses and ashtrays. My Sardarji friend planted himself on the carpet besides Jennifer's feet, looking soulfully at her with his large cocker-spaniel eyes. He rested his head against her thighs and began stroking her shapely legs.

'Please tell your friend to behave himself,' said Jennifer to me.

I spoke to him in Punjabi. He was too far gone to listen to me in any language. Jennifer got up from her chair and sat down in another. After a while the Sardarji hauled himself up, planted himself on the arm of the same chair and began stroking Jennifer's hair. I spoke more sharply this time. It was no use. 'Jennifer, I think you should go to your apartment,' I suggested.

Jennifer only changed her chair. The Sardarji followed her and resumed his ministrations. I lost my temper. 'For God's sake, stop pestering Jennifer! You are drunk. You better go to bed.'

He took no notice of me. It became like a game of hide-and-seek between the two with me playing the role of a referee.

Neither took my advice to retire to their respective beds. Then in the game of chase, the Sardarji slipped and fell. His turban came off and he was sick all over my carpet. I was very angry.

Jennifer apologized and left. I went off to my bedroom and left my house-guest wallowing in his vomit.

The next morning I told my Sardarji friend to find lodgings elsewhere. He left without protest or apology. I wrote a note to Jennifer, apologizing for his behaviour and hoping that she would not drop me because of what had happened. I thought it best not to leave my door open to welcome her when she returned from the theatre and let her, if she wanted, knock at my door. I found a note from her saying not to worry. But she did not knock at my door. Night after night I saw her legs as she alighted from the bus, heard the click of the lock opening the front door and her footsteps going up the stairs. I felt let down and punished for no fault of mine.

And lonely. I could not concentrate on my work. My peace of mind was gone. I felt that if I met my Sardarji friend again I would punch him in the nose for what he had done by ruining a beautiful friendship.

Came next Sunday. Bright and sunny with peals of church bells from distant spires, the loudest being from 'Jennifer's round the corner'. I could not contain myself any more. I decided to go up to her bed-sitting room apartment—she had never invited me—and take her out for a drive into the country as we had done in the past. I was sure she would relent and make up.

I went up the dark stairway to the top floor. Beside the door bell was a strip of paper with the name 'Jennifer Dawson'. I rang the bell. I heard Jennifer's voice shouting, 'See who it is. May be a telegram or something.' The door opened. Facing me stood my Sardarji friend in his pyjamas.

THE RAJNEESH APPROACH
TO SEX

There are many ways of attaining godhood, say teachers of religion. Acharya Rajneesh disagrees and says there is only one way, and sexual intercourse is the first step towards it. He maintains that religion as it is practised, is false, and its propagators are agents of Satan. They have degraded love and taught us the negation of life. The philosophy of religion has always been death-oriented instead of being life-oriented. He goes on to add: 'I call religion the art of living. Religion is not a way to undermine life; it is a medium for delving deeply into the mysteries of existence. Religion is not turning one's back on life; it is facing life squarely. Religion is not escaping from life; religion is embracing life fully. Religion is the total realization of life.'

Since love is the essence of all religions and sex the essence of love, you cannot sidestep it to proceed on your voyage of discovery. Rajneesh writes, 'Sex is the beginning of the journey to love. The origin, the Gangotri of the Ganges of Love, is sex, passion—and everybody behaves like its enemy. Every culture, every religion, every guru, every seer has attacked this Gangotri, this source, and the river has remained bottled up. The hue and cry has always been, "Sex is sin. Sex is irreligious. Sex is poison." But we never seem to realize that ultimately, it is the sex energy itself that travels to and reaches the inner ocean of love. Love is the transformation of sex energy.'

Because sex has been condemned and suppressed, 'it has become an obsession, a disease, a perversion', says the Acharya, and advises us to 'accept sex with joy. Acknowledge its sacredness... When a man approaches his wife he should have a sacred feeling, as if he were going to a temple. And when a wife goes to her husband she should be full of the reverence one has nearing God. In the moments of sex, lovers pass through coitus, and that stage is very near to the temple of God, to where he is manifest in creative formlessness.' He conjectures that man had his first glimpse of samadhi during sexual intercourse culminating in a climax when the mind becomes empty of thoughts. Thus vishyanand (bliss of coitus) and Brahmanand (bliss of union with God) are much the same; one is ephemeral, the other eternal.

Not all sexual intercourse is experience of divinity. For that you have to first get rid of your ego. 'Unless I dissolve myself, how can the other unite with me?' he asks. Love always gives; the ego is ever the grabber; love is motiveless, the ego always motivated; the ego only understands the language of taking; the language of giving is love. The second condition to be fulfilled is the feeling of timelessness. 'In orgasm, the sense of time is non-existent. There is no past, no future, there is only the present moment.'

The Acharya has some practical suggestions to overcome an unhealthy obsession with sexuality. Children should be allowed to remain nude as much as possible in the home so that they do not develop prurient curiosity in private organs. They should also be taught to meditate (on what, he does not say) in silence for at least one hour every day. They should be taught what sex is all about before they are old enough to engage in it. He writes, 'Sex is the most mysterious, most profound, most precious and, at the same time, the most accursed subject; and we are in total darkness about it. We never pay our attention to this important phenomenon. A man goes through the routine of coitus throughout his life, but he does not know what it is.'

The Acharya, who claims to have had sexual fulfilment in his previous life which cleared his mind of sexuality for his present incarnation and those to come, tells us how to get the best out of coitus. Most of us are used to quickies which end in frustration and incite us to have more of the same thing. Coitus, he tells us, must be prolonged as much as possible. In the way of techniques, he suggests slowing down one's breathing and focusing awareness to a point between the eyes, the seat of the agnichakra. If you can prolong intercourse to one hour, you need not think of sex for the rest of your life; if you can prolong it to three hours, you will be liberated from sexuality for your lives to come. A third essential condition is that you should approach sex with reverence. 'Give sex a sacred status in your life,' he says. 'At the time of coitus, we are close to God.'

The Acharya tells us the sculptors of erotica on the temples of Konark, Khajuraho and Puri had the right approach to sex. We should have such temples all over India. Tantriks were also on the right path; preachers of religious dogma suppressed them. He concludes: 'The journey to kama is also the journey to Rama. The journey to lust is also the journey to light. The tremendous attraction for sex is also the search for the sublime.'

It is difficult to decide how seriously one can take Rajneesh. As anything else he writes, his *From Sex to Super-Consciousness* is extremely readable.

Sunday, 12 August 1989

THE VANISHING PENIS

The worldwide obsession with the spread of AIDS seems to me to be vastly exaggerated. No one has yet been able to explain why our ancestors, who practised every form of sexual perversion including sex with animals (for proof visit the Sun Temple, Konark), did not get AIDS, but somehow, African monkeys transmitted them to humans, most of all, the Americans. Also, why some Indians, like some of our esteemed doctors, should warn us against copulating with foreigners because they are more likely to be carriers of this dreaded disease than our own country folk. Mind you, they are careful in limiting their warning to 'visiting foreigners', not those already resident in India or married to Indians. That would be taking matters too far and to the highest quarters.

The AIDS scare is by no means the first of its kind to engulf large sections of the population. From time to time, fear of losing one's manhood has spread like the plague across certain parts of Asia. Two years ago *The San Francisco Chronicle* reported 'the existence of a psychological epidemic that periodically spreads throughout the Far East, sometimes affecting millions of men, whereby males are convinced that their penises are shrinking into their abdomen, and that if this happens they will die'. It went on to add that 'whenever this delusion sweeps across Asia, every decade or two, many men wear bamboo contraptions intended to keep their genitalia from disappearing while they sleep.' The Chinese have actually coined a word for the penis-shrinking phenomenon: koro. And, of course, there is nothing to it; it is the figment of a sick imagination.

Koro is a useful word because the fear of sexual inadequacy in different forms keeps erupting from time to time. The introduction of the birth control pill in the 1960s produced a brand of phobia. So did the aggressive women's lib movement. The more women demanded equality with men in jobs and in bed, the more men felt a sense of inadequacy to meet their demands. So at one end of the spectrum we have the machismo of overconfident males and, at the other, men gnawed by self-doubts. Nothing would dampen the ardour of a person who thinks he is God's gift to womankind, the stud-bull of virility, than to be put down as a victim of 'korophobia'.

Sunday, 24 December 1988

SEX, A PERSONAL VIEWPOINT

As a man gets older, his sexual instincts travel from his groin to his head. What he wanted to do in his younger days but did not because of nervousness, lack of response or opportunity, he does in his mind.

If you ask me what's more important, sex or romance, it's sex. Romance is just a gloss, some sort of sheen that wears off, and it loses its lustre very soon.

I've never really had the time nor the inclination for romance. Romantic interludes take up a lot of time and are a sheer waste of energy, for the end result isn't very much. Sex is definitely more important, though sex with the same person can get boring after a while...you know, routine. Phir wo baat nahin rahti hai... A partner once bedded becomes a bore. Even the best-looking man or woman becomes boring. When it comes to sex, I don't think looks matter much.

I have many women friends. And I also keep in touch with those I've made love to in the past. I can't stand women who are not animated. She could be the most beautiful woman, but if she's not lively, then, as far as I'm concerned, there's no point. I've been with many women over the years. I've never worried about infections or sexually transmitted diseases. You don't think of all this while making love. You just go for it. Once it's up it has to go in there—there's no other way!

I've had affairs that I've used as material for my writing. They contributed to the love-making scenes and passages in my stories and novels. The affairs were very good while they lasted but then you move on, without any unpleasantness. You just drift apart. And in the instances where the women have persisted, I've withdrawn after a point—I've always wanted my space and have never wanted anyone to get too close to me emotionally. I value my space and have guarded it because of my writing. I've never had any close friends or deep emotional relationships. Writing is a solitary task and I'm more comfortable being alone. I get impatient with people and places, so I move on. I've been like this all my life.

I have been with women of almost every nationality and they are the same in bed. Foreigners don't make love differently; their attitude towards love-making might be different. And all those notions about the French being great lovers or that English women are frigid—they are all myths. Years ago, before I'd travelled to England, I had heard that Englishwomen were frigid, cold and reserved. Nothing could be more wrong. That sort of stereotyping—it's absolute rubbish. Nationalities, even religious backgrounds, make no difference at all. It's the desire, the intensity, that's important; there has to be that attraction. Of course, there could be problems if one of the partners has an insatiable appetite and the other has little interest in sex! As far as I'm concerned, I've never been in a situation like this, so I've never really had any awkward moments.

And like nationality or religious background, size does not matter either—whether it's the size of the penis or that of the breasts, whether the lips are full... None of it matters. There just has to be desire on both sides, and reciprocation of feelings. And there should be no suppression or holding back. For if you withhold your urges it will come out in some other form; there's bound to be some aberration. There's far too much sexual frustration in our country and this probably explains the rapes and molestations we hear about every other day. They happen in other countries too, but in India it seems to be a problem now more than ever before. And it's linked to sexual repression and our hypocrisy—we Indians are very interested in sex, we have the curiosity and the drive and we pretend to be prudish and conservative.

I had my first sexual encounter in 1934. I was around nineteen. It was an expectedly unfulfilling encounter with a prostitute from Kamatipura, the red-light district of Bombay. She was fat, dark, middle-aged and dressed in a dirty salwar kameez. I spent myself even as I entered her. The encounter cost me ten rupees.

The first time I saw female genitals it was a sight! It wasn't attractive or appealing at all—on the contrary, it was appalling! Appalling! I was in my teens and there was a lunch being hosted on the lawns of the teacher's quarters in my school. When this lady teacher tried sitting on the grass, her sari rode up and exposed her thighs and much more. That fleeting glimpse of the teacher's private parts had revolted me but it was also then that my curiosity about a woman's body was whetted and I would try and peep when women labourers were bathing semi-clad... It was with that glimpse that I first became aware of desire.

Another time, when I was recovering from yet another bout of typhoid, a nurse hired to look after me went beyond her call of duty—she did more than sponge my body. I was still young, in my teens, but that didn't deter her from holding my penis and even kissing it. I was too young to know what was happening, and also too weak and too ill to respond, react or enjoy it.

And long before that, when I was a young child, a cousin tried exploring my body. She must have been around the same age as I was, yet we'd tried touching each other and somehow it aroused something—a strange curiosity about the female form.

I don't think it's only men who seduce. I find that women are often better at the art of seduction. More than me trying to seduce women, it's women who've tried seducing me all these years. Right from the beginning—the very first time I was attracted to a woman, it was she who took the first move—she held my hand in the cinema hall. Even later, with other women too, it was the women, with the exception of one or two cases, who made a pass first, leading me on. I have rarely taken the lead. When I've been attracted to someone, I've had little confidence in expressing myself. And years later, when I happened to tell them how I'd felt, several of them exclaimed, 'Why the hell didn't you tell me before?' Each time I've had a woman make a pass at me I've felt flattered and have reciprocated. Looking back I wish I'd had the confidence to make the first move.

JEFFREY ARCHER AND THE
PROSTITUTE

The Jeffrey Archer Libel Case going on in England has been cursorily noticed in our papers. By the time you get to read this, the verdict will be known. Nevertheless I'll give you a brief background before I explain why I am writing about it. Archer, forty-seven, is a best-selling author, father of two children, former deputy chairman of the Conservative Party in Parliament and a friend of Mrs Thatcher. One evening last year he accosted Monica Coghlan (Debbie to her clients) in Shepherd's Market, an upper-class prostitute area in London's Mayfair. He agreed to pay Debbie her fee of £50 and went to fetch his car. Meanwhile, Debbie had a quickie with an old client, a Turk named Kurtha, who was practising as a solicitor in London. Kurtha recognized Archer and remarked, 'Debbie, you've hit the jackpot. That's Jeffrey Archer, the rich author and Member of Parliament.' Since Debbie didn't read newspapers or books, the name meant nothing to her. She collected her honorarium, did her job, and offered a repeat performance for £20 which was rejected.

Kurtha leaked the information to *Private Eye* and then to Star and *News of the World*. Press hounds smelt blood and persuaded Debbie to ring up Archer and ask for more money because newspapermen were after her. The fool tried to buy her off with an offer of £2,000 to go abroad. The conversation was taped. The papers paid Debbie thousands of pounds for her story and splashed it across their front pages. Archer was left with no option but to deny the story, plead alibi on the evening concerned and sue for libel to clear his name. His counsel, Robert Alexander QC, tried to impugn Debbie's evidence by suggesting that a woman who, without telling her family had taken to whoring since she was eighteen, must be 'a very accomplished liar'. While admitting that she had had sex with thousands of men, Debbie resolutely denied that she had developed a dislike for the male sex. 'I enjoy my job. As long as men are all right with me, I am all right with them,' she said.

This brings me to the issues on which I would like to comment. Debbie was asked, 'You would guess that many of the men who come to you are married men?'

'Most of them.'

'They are all looking for sex away from their wives, often in sordid hotels?'

'Well, what's wrong with that?'

'After all that, you have respect for the male sex?'

'Yes, I do. Perhaps half of the time it keeps marriages together.'

I asked myself three questions: Must it be assumed that a prostitute, because she keeps her family in ignorance about her profession, lies about everything else? Is it true that married men consort with prostitutes more than bachelors do? And does occasional extramarital sex really help in keeping marriages together?

I think it is extremely unfair to equate a prostitute with a liar. Politicians indulge in lying much more than harlots, and with less excuse. A prostitute performs a necessary social function in society and is more vital for its stability than professions such as politics, law or journalism. She keeps her family in the dark about her means of livelihood only to save them from social stigma, but in other dealings she can be as straight as a saadhvi.

I am also inclined to agree with Debbie on her other two points: that the majority of patrons of prostitutes are married men, and occasional sex with a whore does not destroy a marriage. Although I have utter contempt for men who pay for their pleasures, I concede that if they feel compelled to engage in extramarital affairs, it is better that they go to an anonymous person like a prostitute than get embroiled with someone who will inevitably make demands on their emotions. It is the extramarital love affair that destroys a marriage, not extramarital sex with a prostitute. It remains to be seen how the Archers weather the storm of publicity that has broken over their heads.

Sunday, 8 August 1987

THE SECRET TO LASTING LONG

There are no clearly defined borders between youth, middle and old age. Some young men and women become middle-aged in their thirties, others remain young in their fifties and sixties; some become impotent in their youth, others continue to enjoy sex into their eighties. Indeed, most people will agree that as long as you are capable of enjoying sex, you are young; when the sexual urge disappears, you have become old. Men are more obsessed with proving their potency than women and, when natural impulses begin to wane, will try all kinds of aphrodisiacs to keep going. Unfortunately for them, so far, medical science has not produced any reliable sex rejuvenants. Good health and worldly success are more potent than any kushta. Henry

Kissinger was hundred per cent right when he said that power is the ultimate aphrodisiac. So we find so many successful politicians compulsive womanizers. Equally potent is the company of the young and the vivacious.

Sexual urges are generated by hormones secreted by the pituitary gland located beneath the brain, the testes and, in the case of women, in the ovaries. These age with the aging of their owners. Also, in monogamous marriages, the absence of variety—which is indeed the spice of life when it comes to sex—and monotony deprive both partners of the urge to engage in lovemaking. Statistics show that in marriages which have lasted more than twenty years, the sex urge has all but disappeared. Attempts to revive it with the same partner are not successful, but failure to do so does not impair matrimonial closeness. Men in their fifties and sixties are still capable of sex once a week. The urge tapers off in the seventies and is usually extinct in the eighties.

But both men and women hanker after sex even after the natural urge has abated. The natural way to prolong the sex urge are liaisons with younger people. Aging men are drawn towards girls younger than their daughters and young girls respond to overtures of men who become their father figures. Likewise, older women take on young lovers who see in them their mother-mistresses. The relationships are utterly Freudian, utterly unnatural, but utterly fulfilling for both partners even if the sex in the relationships is not satisfactory.

One sure way to impotence is to ignore the presence of attractive members of the opposite sex. Men and women who take to religion in their later lives and spend most of their time in the company of their own age group age prematurely and lose the zest for living.

For those anxious to revive their sex lives, there are hormone injections which revive potency for fifteen days. Most pathetic are cases of men who have the desire but are unable to perform. Even for them medical science has found stuff to inject into their genitals to revive them. Experiments are afoot to produce a pill which will have the same effect.

Heavy drinking over many years can have disastrous effects on male or female potency. Alcohol may temporarily whip up desire, but it robs the drinker of the power to perform. Fortunately, most drinking men in their late seventies and eighties, if given the choice between a willing female and a slug of premium Scotch, will opt for the latter.

The Hindustan Times, 10 February 1996

KISSING

Some years ago I took the liberty of greeting the then Pakistani high commissioner Ashraf Jehangir Qazi's daughter with a kiss. She was around sixteen; I, nearing ninety. Her grandfather and granduncle were in college with me in England. A photograph of my embracing the teenager appeared in *The Indian Express* and was picked up by some Pakistani papers. It created a furore in Pakistan. Qazi was summoned to Islamabad to explain his daughter's conduct. He did so to their satisfaction. They felt pretty foolish about it. There were two postscripts to the event.

A few days later, a Pakistani family, including their young daughters, came to call on me. As I opened the door to welcome them, the father said to me, 'First, give my daughters a kiss, then we will come in.' And before the Qazis left India for USA, they came to say goodbye to me. This time it was their daughter who took the initiative, put her arms round my neck and kissed me on both my bearded cheeks. I often wonder what would have happened if instead of Qazi's little girl, I had taken the same liberty with her grandaunt, Pyari Begam, who was a great beauty and was in my age group. Perhaps it would have led to a war between the Baluchis and the Sikhs. It was truly said by Don Marquis: 'Mayhem, death and arson have followed many a thoughtless kiss not sanctioned by a person.'

There are a number of ways of kissing: an avuncular on the forehead, the fraternal on both cheeks, the more intricate on the lips, or side of the neck. The choice largely depends on the female recipient because males are over-eager to convert the gesture into an intimate relationship. It is said high-heeled shoes were specially invented for short women who were tired of being kissed on their foreheads. An honest kiss demands the meeting of the lips. Even with this, there are countless ways of expressing the range of emotions.

Vatsayan made a list of over sixty ways in his sex classic *Kama Sutra*. In the matter of kissing, no one needs a textbook to guide him or her. They know all there is to know from the day they were born. Nor do they have to wait for astral signs to tell them of auspicious days to go ahead. There is an old English saying: 'Kissing is not in season when the gorse is not in bloom.' Gorse is in full blossom right through the year. It grows in profusion in the Shivaliks: it is a foot-high bush with tiny pink flowers.

One does not have to define a kiss. Henry Gibbons made a silly attempt which robbed it of all the joy it yields, to wit: 'The anatomised juxtaposition of two orbicularis oris muscles in a state of contraction.' Nonsense. The poet Robert Herrick was much closer to the mark when he wrote: 'What is a kiss? Why kiss, as some approve; they pave sweet cement, glue and lime of love.'

Kisses can be lethal as well as life-giving. There was the Kiss of Judas which betrayed Jesus Christ and led to his crucifixion. It was the kiss of death. There is also the prolonged kiss of resuscitation to save the life of a drowned person. There is the kiss that reveals a past relationship. There is a kiss which means nothing but the meeting of lips as an old Italian proverb says: 'A kiss on the lip does not always touch the heart.' It is the kind of kiss that film actors plant on each other under the glare of lights in front of cameras with dozens of people watching them. These are fake emotions that don't exist. Meanwhile, I find solace in an old Spanish saying: 'A kiss without a moustache is like an egg without salt.' I have plenty of moustache.

A MEMORABLE TRAIN JOURNEY

Many winters ago I happened to be travelling by a night train from Delhi to Bhopal. It was an express that made a few halts at major stations. I found myself in a compartment of five berths: three below and two on the sides above. I had a lower berth as did the other two passengers who were there before me. The upper berths were reserved in the names of Professor and Mrs Saxena. Fifteen minutes before the train was due to leave, a party of men and women escorting a bride decked in an ornate sari drawn discreetly across her face and her arm loaded with ivory bangles stopped by our compartment, read the names on the panel and came in. They were dismayed to see the two berths reserved for them separated by a fifteen-foot chasm of space. One of the party approached me and asked if I could take one of the upper berths to accommodate the newlyweds. I readily agreed and moved my bedding roll. Another passenger who had the middle berth also moved up on the other upper berth so that the bridal couple could be alongside each other. I heard one of the party stop the conductor and tell him to wake up the couple at a particular junction where the train was to make a brief three-minute halt at 3 a.m.

As the conductor blew his whistle and waved his green flag, the party took leave of the bridal couple with much embracing and sobbing. No sooner had the train cleared the lighted platform than the bride blew her nose and uncovered her face. She was in her mid-twenties: pale-skinned, round-faced and wearing thick glasses. I couldn't see much of her figure but my guess was that she would be forever fighting a losing battle against fat. Her groom looked a couple of years older than her (the 'professor' being honorific for a junior lecturer) and like his bride, was sallow-faced, corpulent and bespectacled. From the snatches of conversation that I could hear (I was only four feet above them), I gathered that they were total strangers and their marriage had been arranged by relatives and through the matrimonial columns of the *Hindustan Times*. They talked of their papajis and mummyjis. Then of their time in college (the halcyon days for most educated Indians) and of their friends: 'like a brother to me' or 'better than my own real sister'. After a while the conversation began to flag; I saw the man's hand resting on his woman's, on the windowsill.

The lights were switched off leaving only a nightlight which bathed the compartment in a moonlight blue. I could not see very much except when the train ran past brightly lit platforms of wayside railway stations.

The couple did not bother to use the middle berth vacated for them and decided to make themselves as comfortable as they could on a four-foot wide wooden plank. They ignored the presence of the other passengers in the small compartment and were totally absorbed in getting to know each other. Such was their impatience that they did not find the time to change into more comfortable clothes. They drew a quilt over themselves and were lost to the world.

The sari is a costume that is both very ornamental as well as functional. Properly draped, it can accentuate the contours of the female form, giving a special roundness to the buttocks. A well-cut blouse worn with the sari elevates the bosom and exposes the belly to below the navel. There is no other form of female attire which can both conceal physical shortcomings of the wearer as well as expose what deserves exposure. A fat woman looks less fat in a sari than she would in a dress, and a thin woman looks more filled in. At the same time, a sari is very functional. All a woman has to do when she wants to urinate or defecate is to lift it to her waist. When required to engage in a quick sexual intercourse, she needs to do no more than draw it up a little and open up her thighs. Apparently this was what Mrs Saxena was called upon to do. I heard a muffled cry of 'Hai Ram' escape her lips and realized that the marriage had been consummated.

The Saxenas did not get up to go to the bathroom to wash themselves but began a repeat performance. This time they were less impatient and seemed to be getting more out of their efforts. More than once the quilt slipped off them and I caught a glimpse of the professor's heaving buttocks and his bride's bosoms which he had extricated out of her choli. Above the rattle and whish of the speeding train I heard the girl's whimper and the man's exulting grunts. They had a third go at each other before peace descended on our compartment. It was then well past midnight. Thereafter it was only the wail of the engine tearing through the dark night and the snores of my elderly companions that occasionally disturbed my slumber.

We were rudely woken by someone thumping on the door, slapping the window panes and yelling, 'Get up! Get up! It is Sehore. The train will leave in another minute.' It was the conductor.

I turned the switch on and the compartment was flooded with light. A memorable sight it was! Professor Saxena fast asleep with his buttocks exposed; Mrs Saxena also fast asleep, her mouth wide open, breasts bare, lying supine like a butterfly pinned on a board. Her hair was scattered on her pillow. Their glasses lay on the floor.

Whatever embarrassment they felt was drowned in the hustle and bustle of getting off the train. We heaved out their beds and suitcases. The professor stumbled out onto the cold platform adjusting his flies. His wife followed him covering her bare bosom with a flap of her sari. As the train began to move, she screamed— one of her earrings was missing. The friendly guard brought the train to a halt. All of us went down on our knees scouring the floor. The errant earring was found wedged in a crevice of the seat. We resumed our journey.

'It is love,' remarked one of my travelling companions with great understanding. 'They are newly married and this was their first night together. All should be forgiven for people in love.'

'What kind of love?' I asked in a sarcastic tone. 'A few hours ago they were complete strangers. They haven't the patience to wait till they get home; they start having sex without as much as exchanging a word of affection. You call that love?'

'Well,' he replied pondering over the episode. 'They may not get another chance for some days. There will be his relatives, his mother, sisters, brothers. And lots of religious ceremonies. Youth is impatient and the body has its own compulsions. Let us say it is the beginning of love.'

'It may be the beginning of another family, but I don't see where love comes in,' I remarked. 'I can understand illiterate peasants coupling like the cattle they rear, but I cannot understand two educated people—a lecturer in a college and a school teacher—lacking so totally in sophistication or sense of privacy as to begin copulating in the presence of three strangers.'

'You have foreign ideas,' said the third man, dismissing me. 'Anyway, it is 3.30 in the morning. Let's get some sleep.' He switched off the light and the argument.

The episode stayed in my mind because it vividly

illustrated the pattern of the man-woman relationship that is common among the vast majority of Indians. Love as the word is understood in the West is known only to a tiny minority of the very Westernized living in the half-a-dozen big cities of India, who prefer to speak English rather than Indian languages, read only English books, watch only Western movies and even dream in English. For the rest, it is something they read about in poems or see on the screen but very rarely experience personally. Arranged marriages are the accepted norm; 'love' marriages, a rarity. In arranged marriages, the parties first make each other's acquaintance physically through the naked exploration of each other's bodies, and it is only after some of the lust has been drained out of their systems that they get the chance to discover each other's minds and personalities. It is only after lust begins to lose its potency and there is no clash of temperaments that the alliance may, in later years, develop bonds of companionship. But the chances of this happening are bleak. In most cases, they suffer each other till the end of their days.

I have no idea what became of the Saxenas whose nuptial consummation I had been witness to. It is likely that by now they had produced a small brood of Saxenas. He is probably a full professor teaching romantic poetry and occasionally penning a verse or two to some younger lady professor ('like a sister to me') or to some pig-tailed student ('like my own daughter'). Mrs Saxena probably tries to retain her husband's interest through dog-like devotion and prayer and with the help of charms brought from 'holy' men. On the rare occasions when the professor mounts her, she has to fantasize about one of his younger colleagues ('exactly like a real brother to me') before she shudders in the throes of an orgasm with the name of God on her lips—'Hai Ram'.

The Saxenas are luckier than most Indian couples because they live away from their families and are assured a certain amount of privacy. To most newly married Indian couples, the concept of privacy is as alien as that of love. They rarely get a room to themselves; the bride-wife sleeps with women members of her husband's family; the husband shares his charpoy placed alongside his father's and brothers'. Occasionally the mother-in-law, anxious to acquire a grandson, will contrive a meeting between her son and his wife: the most common technique is to get her to take a tumbler of milk to the lad when other male members are elsewhere. The lad grabs the chance for the 'quickie'. Hardly ever does the couple get enough time for a prolonged and satisfying bout of intercourse. Most

Indian men are not even aware that women also have orgasms; most Indian women share this ignorance because although they go from one pregnancy to another, they have no idea that sex can be pleasurable. This is a sad commentary on the people of the country that produced the most widely read treatise on the art of sex, the *Kama Sutra*, and elevated the act of sex to spiritual sublimity by explicit depictions on its temples.

A MIXED MARRIAGE

I was born in 633 Hijri corresponding to the year 1265 of the Christian calendar. It was the beginning of the reign of Sultan Ghiasudddin Balban. My ancestors had been scribes in the service of the rulers of Delhi. They had served Raja Anangpal, the Tomara Rajput, who built Lal Kot and planted the sacred iron pillar of Vishnu Bhagwan in the middle of the city. They had also served Raja Prithvi Raj Chauhan who renamed the city Qila Rai Pithoras. When Mohammed Ghori defeated and slew Raja Prithvi Raj and became ruler of Delhi my ancestors acquired knowledge of Turki, Arabic and Persian and continued in the service of the new ruler. My great-grandfather served under Sultan Qutubuddin Aibak and with his own eyes saw the destruction of

Hindu and Jain temples, the building of the Jama Masjid, later called Quwwat-ul-Islam, on their ruins and the beginnings of the tower of victory, the Qutub Minar. My grandfather served under Qutubuddin's son-in-law and successor Sultan Altamash. Like a common labourer he dug the earth for the Shamsi Talab at the site where the Sultan had seen footprints of the Holy Prophet's horse, Buraq, and carried stones on his head to build the mausoleum of the Saint Qutubuddin Bakhtiyar Kaki. He saw the Qutub Minar completed in AD 1220. It was my grandfather who built the stone house along the Shamsi Talab where I was born and spent most of my life. He also served under Sultan Altamash's daughter Razia Sultana who ruled over Hindustan for three-and-a-half years. My father, Lala Chagan Lal, was a clerk in the Kotwali (police station) of Mehrauli under the mighty Sultan Ghiasuddin Balban and served him for fifteen of the twenty years of his reign which lasted from 1265 AD to 1287 AD. (My father died in the year 1280 AD.)

Like my Kayastha forefathers, I was trained to be a scribe. A pandit taught me Sanskrit and Hindi. Through my father's influence I was admitted to a madrasa to learn Arabic, Turki and Persian. At first I was treated roughly by the Turkish boys and sons of Hindu converts to Islam. But when I learnt to speak Turki and dress like a Turk, they stopped bullying me. To save me from being harassed, the Maulvi Sahib gave me a Muslim name, Abdul. The boys called me Abdullah.

I was the only child of my parents. I had been betrothed to a girl, one of a family of seven who lived in Mathura. We were married when I was nine and my wife, Ram Dulari, only seven. Four years later, when I was old enough to cohabit, my parents sent the barber who had arranged my marriage to fetch my wife from Mathura. For reasons I will explain later, her parents refused to comply with our wishes. Then tragedy struck our home. My father died and a few days later my mother joined him. At thirteen I was left alone in the world.

The Kotwal Sahib was very kind to me. When he came to offer his condolence, he also offered my father's post to me.

It was at that time my Muslim friends suggested that if I accepted conversion to Islam my prospects would be brighter; I could even aspire to become Kotwal of Mehrauli. And I would have no trouble in finding a wife from amongst the new converts. If I was lucky I might even get a widow or a divorcee of pure Turkish, Persian or Afghan stock. 'If you are Muslim,' said one fellow who was full of witticisms, 'you can have any woman you like. If you are up to it, you can have four at a time.'

A Turk for toughness, for hands that never tire;
An Indian for her rounded bosom bursting with
    milk;
A Persian for her tight crotch and her coquetry;
An Uzbeg to thrash as a lesson for the three.

There was something, I do not know what, which held me back from being converted to Islam. I suspected that the reason why my wife's parents had refused to send her to me was the rumour that my parents had adopted the ways of the Mussalmans. If I became a Muslim, they would say, 'Didn't we tell you? How could we give our daughter to an unclean maleecha?'

On the last day of the obsequial ceremony for my mother, my wife's uncle came from Mathura to condole with me. His real object was to find out what I was like and whether I observed Hindu customs. With his own eyes he saw that I had my head shaved, wore the sacred thread and fed Brahmins. I asked the barber to speak to him about sending my wife to me. The uncle did not say anything and returned to Mathura.

After waiting for some days I approached the Kotwal Sahib.

At that time people felt that fate had dealt harshly with me and were inclined to be sympathetic. The Kotwal Sahib made me write out a complaint against my wife's parents for interfering with my conjugal rights. He forwarded it to the Kotwal of Mathura with a recommendation for immediate execution. If the family raised any objection, they were to be arrested and sent to Mehrauli.

A week later my wife, escorted by her younger sister and uncle, arrived at my doorstep. After a few days her uncle and sister returned to Mathura.

Ram Dulari behaved in a manner becoming a Hindu wife. She touched my feet every morning and wore vermilion powder in the parting of her hair. But she cried all the time and if I as much as put my arm on her shoulder to comfort her she shrank away from me. One night when I went to her bed she started to scream. Our neighbour woke up and shouted across the roof to ask if all was well. I felt very foolish.

Even after one month I did not know what she looked like because she kept her face veiled with the end of her dupatta. It was only from her neck and hands that I made out that she was fair. I also noticed that her bosom was full and her buttocks nicely rounded.

It took me several weeks to realize that my wife did

not intend to cohabit with me. She cooked her food on a separate hearth and ate out of utensils she had brought with her. For her I was an unclean Muslim maleecha. I tried to take her by force. I beat her. It was no use. I asked her whether she would like to return to her parents. She said that she would only go if I threw her out or when she was taken away on her bier. What was I to do? Could I go to the Kotwal Sahib and ask him to order my wife to spread her legs for me! Gradually, I reconciled myself to my fate. We slept under the same roof but never on the same charpoy.

One morning I took Ram Dulari to see the Qutub Minar. We climbed up to the first storey and I pointed out the mausoleum of the Saint Qutubuddin Bakhtiyar Kaki, the Auliya Masjid alongside the Shamsi Talab, our own little home on the other side.

And right below us the tomb of Sultan Altamash. I showed her the slab on which a Hindu stonemason had inscribed 'Sri Visvakarme Prasade Rachita' and stuck it into this Muslim tower of victory. We came down and I took her towards the Quwwat-ul-Islam mosque. I explained to her how the Turks had demolished twenty-seven Hindu and Jain temples and buried the idols of Vishnu and Lakshmi beneath the entrance gate so that Muslims going in to pray could trample on them. She refused to enter the mosque. As we were retracing our steps, she noticed that the figures of Hindu gods and goddesses on the pillars of what had once been a Hindu temple had been mutilated: noses sliced off, arms broken, breasts chopped off. She put her head against a pillar and began to cry. A small crowd collected. I pretended she was not feeling well and pushed her along. If it hadn't been for the fact that I was dressed like a Mussalman and my wife wore a burqa (all Hindu women of rank wore burqas) it could have been very awkward. When we got home I reprimanded her very severely.

The Hindus' hatred of the Mussalmans did not make sense to me. The Muslims had conquered Hindustan. Why hadn't our gods saved us from them? There was that Sultan Mahmud of Ghazni who had invaded Hindustan seventeen times—not once or twice but seventeen times. He had destroyed the temple of Chakraswamy at Thanesar and nothing happened to him. Then Somnath. They said that even the sea prostrated itself twice every twenty-four hours to touch the feet of Somnath. But even the sea did not rise to save Somnathji from Mahmud. They said that Mahmud used to chop off the fingers of the Hindu rajas he defeated in battle; his treasury was full of Hindu fingers.

He styled himself as Yaminuddaulah—the right hand of God; and Zill-e-Illahi—the Shadow of God on earth.

The Muslims had become masters of Hindustan. They were quite willing to let us Hindus live our lives as we wanted to, provided we recognized them as our rulers. But the Hindus were full of foolish pride. 'This is our country!' they said. 'We will drive out these cow-killers and destroyers of our temples.' They were especially contemptuous towards Hindus who had embraced Islam and treated them worse than untouchables.

The Hindus lived on the stale diet of past glory. At every gathering they talked of the great days of the Tomaras and the Chauhans.

'Arrey bhai! Who can deny our ancients were great!' I told my Hindu friends a hundred times. 'But let us think of today. We cannot fight the Mussalmans; they are too big, too strong and too warlike for us. Let us be sensible and learn to live in peace with them.' But reason never entered the skull of the Hindu. Everyone in the world knows that if you put the four Vedas on one side of the scale and commonsense on the other commonsense will be heavier. But not so with the Hindus. They would look contemptuously at me and call me a pimp of the Mussalmans. Their great hero was

Prithivi Raj Chauhan who had defeated Ghori once at Tarain in 1191 AD. But the very next year, on the same battlefield, he had been defeated and slain by the same Ghori. They had an answer to that too. 'Prithvi Raj's only mistake was to spare the life of the maleecha when he had first defeated him,' they would reply. Nobody really knows the truth about this Prithvi Raj. A poet fellow named Chand Bardai had made a big song-and-dance about him. This great hero Prithvi Raj married lots of women and even abducted the daughter of a neighbouring raja. But you could not say a word against him to the Hindus. Next to Sri Ramchandraji, it was Samrat Prithvi Raj Chauhan who they worshipped.

I realized that I belonged neither to the Hindus nor to the Mussalmans. How could I explain to my wife that while the Brahmins lived on offerings made to their gods, the Rajputs and the Jats had their lands, Aheers and the Gujars their cattle, the Banias their shops, all that the poor Kayasthas had were their brains and their reed pens! And the only people who could pay for their brains and their pens were the rulers who were Muslims!

I was disowned by the Hindus and shunned by my own wife. I was exploited by the Muslims who disdained my company. Indeed, I was like a hijda, who was neither one thing nor another but could be misused by everyone.

Then I heard of Nizamuddin. 'Go to the dervish of Ghiaspur on the bank of the river Jamuna and all your troubles will be over,' people said. They called him auliya (prophet) and also Khwaja Sahib. But there were many learned Mussalmans who called him an imposter who would soon meet the fate he deserved. As becomes a good Kayastha I did not express any opinion and waited to see which way the wind was blowing.

In due course this Nizamuddin was summoned by the Sultan to answer charges of heresy levelled against him. On the day of the trail I took leave from my job and went to the palace.

The very name of Ghiasuddin Balban made people urinate with fear. He had a terrible temper and was known to execute anyone who as much as raised his eyes to look at him. He kept two huge Negroes beside him to hack off the heads of people he sentenced to death.

What a sight it was! The great Sultan on his couch flanked by his Abyssinian bodyguards; black djinns with drawn swords! Hundreds of bearded Turkish generals! On one side of the throne-couch stood five ulema dressed in fine silks. Facing them on the other side was a young man not much older than I. He wore a long shirt of coarse black wool and had a green scarf tied round his head. With him were three of his followers dressed as poorly as he. This was Nizamuddin, the Sufi dervish of Ghiaspur.

The Sultan first addressed Nizamuddin. 'Dervish, the ulema have complained that you make no distinction between Mussalmans and infidels; that you pose as an intermediary between God and man; that you use words which obliterate the difference between man and his Maker; that your followers indulge in music and dancing in the precincts of the mosque and thus contravene the holy law of the shariat. What do you have to say in your defence?'

Nizamuddin smiled and replied: 'O mighty Sultan, it is true that I do not make any distinction between Mussalmans and Hindus as I consider both to be the children of God. The ulema exhort Your Majesty in the name of the Holy Messenger (upon Whom be peace) to destroy temples and slay infidels to gain merit in the eyes of Allah. I interpret the sacred law differently. I believe that the best way to serve God is through love of his creatures. As for the charge of posing as an intermediary between man and his Maker, I plead guilty. God's Messenger (on Whom be peace) said: "Whoever dies without an Imam dies the death of a pagan." We Sufis follow this precept and believe that he who has no Shaikh is without religion. The ulema know not that God often manifests himself in His creatures. They also do not know that Allah cannot be understood through knowledge of books or through logic. His Messenger (peace upon Him) when asked whether even he did not know God replied, "No, not even I. God is an experience."'

The Sultan nodded towards the ulema. Their leader went down on his knees and kissed the ground in front of the throne. 'Jahan Panah (Refuge of the World),' he addressed the Sultan, 'you who are the wisest and the most just of all monarchs do not need such insects as we are to expound the holy law. Your Majesty must know that this man, Nizamuddin, talks of love only to throw dust in the eyes of innocent people.' He unwrapped a copy of the *Quran*, touched it to his forehead, and read out a passage. The crowd broke into a chorus of applause 'Wah! Wah! Subhan Allah!' Few of them understood Arabic. Even fewer understood what the words meant when translated into Turki.

The Sultan turned to the dervish and asked him about his claiming unity with God. Nizamuddin replied in very poetic language, 'O Sultan! And O you ulema learned of the law! And all of you people assembled here! Do you know what it is to love and be loved? Perhaps all you have known and enjoyed is the love of women. We Sufis love God and no one else. When we are possessed by the divine spirit we utter words which to the common man may sound like the assumption of godhood. But these should not be taken seriously. You may have heard of the story of the dove that would not submit to her mate. In his passion the male bird said, "If you do not give in to me, I shall turn the throne of Solomon upside down." The breeze carried his words to Solomon. He summoned the dove and asked it to explain itself. The dove replied, "O Prophet of Allah! The words of lovers should not be bandied about." The answer pleased Solomon. We hope our answer will please the Sultan Balban.'

A murmur of Wah! Wah! went round.

The Sultan asked the ulema for authority on the subject of music. The ulema opened another book (they had brought many bundles of books with them.) Their leader again read out something in Arabic and then translated it into Turki. He looked back at the crowd and a section applauded Wah! Wah!

The Sultan again turned to Nizamuddin. The dervish had not brought any books. From memory he quoted a tradition of the Prophet about music and dancing. 'When Allah's grace enters one's person it manifests itself by making that person sing and dance with joy. If this be a manifestation of being possessed by Allah, I say Amen.'

The Sultan pondered over the matter for a while. He brushed his beard and examined the hair that came off in his hand. The silence was terrible. At last he cleared his throat and spoke in a clear, loud voice. 'We dismiss the ulema's charges against Nizamuddin, dervish of Ghiaspur.'

The crowd broke into loud applause praising the Sultan's sense of justice. Many rushed to the dervish and kissed the hem of his coarse, woollen shirt.

The next morning I asked the Kotwal Sahib about Nizamuddin. 'He's gone up there,' he replied pointing up to the sky. 'He has shown many infidels the true path. Go to him any Thursday or on the eve of the new moon and you'll see what miracles he can perform!'

The following Thursday I hired an ekka to go to Ghiaspur which was more than a kos from Mehrauli. When I got to the hospice and asked an attendant whether I could see the man who was at the palace some days earlier, he replied, 'Khwaja Sahib is meditating in his cell. He only receives visitors in the evening. You can go and eat the langar (free kitchen.)

131

I went to the langar. It was crowded with Muslims and Hindus, rich and poor, clamouring for a leaf-cup of lentils and a morsel of coarse bread. I had to fight my way through the crowd to grab a chappati. I came out and sat in the courtyard where a party of qawwals were singing in Hindi. I was told that the song had been written and composed by one Abdul Hassan, who was very close to the holy man.

Late in the afternoon word went round that the dervish had emerged from his cell. People buzzed round him like bees round a crystal of sugar. I pushed my way through the throng and when I got to him I kissed the hem of his shirt. Suddenly, tears came gushing into my eyes. The dervish put his hand on my head. I felt a tingling sensation run down my spine and the fragrance of musk enveloping my frame. He tilted my tear-stained face upwards and said, 'Just as Allah has let my tunic drink your tears, so may he make your sorrows mine!' As he spoke those words I felt as light as a piece of thistledown floating in the air.

'Abdullah, my son,' he continued, 'you live near the mausoleum of Hazrat Qutubuddin Bakhtiyar Kaki. Go there every morning and recite the ninety-nine names of Allah. Your wishes will be granted. Come whenever your heart is heavy. The doors of our hut of poverty are never bolted against anyone.'

It was on my way back to Mehrauli that I asked myself, 'How does he know that I live near the mausoleum of Bakhtiyar Kaki? How does he know that my Muslim friends call me Abdullah? And if somebody has told him who I am and where I live, how is it that he does not know that I am a Hindu and may not know the ninety-nine names of Allah?'

I could not contain myself. Since there was no one else I could unburden myself to, I told my wife all that had passed. For the first time since we had been married, Ram Dulari showed some interest in me. When I ran out of words she asked very timidly, 'Why don't you take me along one day?' In my enthusiasm I took her hand. It went limp in my grasp.

On the first day of the new month of the Muslim lunar calendar I took Ram Dulari to Ghiaspur. Our ekka was one in a long line on the dusty road. We passed bullock carts loaded with women and children, the men striding along barefoot with their shoes hung on their staves.

There was an immense crowd. A whole bazaar of bangle-sellers, sweet-meat vendors, cloth-dealers and medicine-sellers had gone up. I feared Ram Dulari would not get a chance to have darshan of the holy man. I did not take her to the langar as she should not touch anything cooked by Muslims. We wandered round the stalls, watched jugglers and acrobats, dancing bears and monkeys. We sat down under a tree. I began to despair. In an hour the sun would set and the ekka-driver would insist that we return to Mehrauli before it became dark. I was lost in my thoughts when a dervish came to me and said: 'Abdul! Isn't your name Abdul or Abdullah? The Khwaja Sahib has been enquiring after you.' He led us through a door at the back of the mosque into a courtyard where the holy man was receiving visitors. The dervish forced his way through the crowd with us following close on his heels.

I kissed the hem of the holy man's shirt. Ram Dulari prostrated herself on the ground before him. Khwaja Sahib stretched his hand and blessed her. 'Child, Allah will fulfil your heart's desire. If He wills your womb will bear fruit. Go in peace.' That was all. The crowd pushed us away.

Her womb bear fruit? This man of God who was said to read people's minds like a book had not read Ram Dulari's. From the way she turned away her face I could tell she was embarrassed. On the way back to Mehrauli she avoided touching me. We got off opposite the Auliya Masjid. We walked home as if we had nothing to do with each other. I in front looking at the shuttered doors of shops as if I had never seen them before; she behind me enveloped in her burqa.

As soon as we stepped into our courtyard she lit the hearth to warm up food she had cooked in the morning. I lit an oil lamp in the niche and wrote down the events of the day. She gave me my meal and went back to the kitchen to eat hers. After I had finished I gave her my empty brass plate and went to the bazaar to get a paan-leaf.

By the time I came back Ram Dulari had rinsed the utensils and was lying on her charpoy with her face towards the wall. I blew out the oil-lamp and stretched myself on my charpoy. I could not sleep. I kept thinking about the holy man's promise that we would have children. How could Ram Dulari have them unless I gave them to her? I wondered if she was thinking the same thing. After an hour of turning from side to side I called softly to her, 'Ram Dulari!'

'Hun!'

'Are you asleep?'

'No.'

The gong of the kotwali struck the hour of midnight. Once again I asked Ram Dulari if she was asleep; she said 'No'. Something said she might not be averse to my touching her. I got up and went over to her charpoy. 'Can I lie with you? I asked, 'I feel cold.'

She made room for me and replied, 'If you wish.'

I lay beside her. The passion that I had stored up over the months welled in my body. Just as a torrent carries away everything that comes in its way my lust swept aside my fears. I fell on her like a hungry lion. I tore away her sari and tried to enter her. She spread out her thighs to receive me. But no sooner did I reach between them than my seed was spent. I felt ashamed of myself.

Ram Dulari got up to clean herself. She poured water from the pitcher into her brass lota. She put aside her sari and began to splash water between her thighs. Under the light of the stars I saw her pale body, the outlines of her rounded breasts and her broad hips. She dried herself with the same sari and wrapped it round her body. She hesitated, not sure which charpoy to go to. I stretched out my hand to her. She took it and let me pull her beside me. My passion was roused again. She let me remove her damp sari and warm her naked flesh in my embrace. This time I was able to hold myself longer. And she more eager to receive me. A cry of pain escaped her lips. I knew that I had at long last made Ram Dulari mine.

I re-lit the oil-lamp and helped her wash the stains of blood on the bedsheet. By the time we had finished, our bodies were again hungry for each other. So passed the whole night.

I was woken by the sun on my face and flies buzzing in my ears.

Ram Dulari had bathed and cooked the morning meal. She was wearing the red sari she had worn when she had come to Mehrauli as a bride. She did not cover her face against me and blushed as she saw me get up from her bed. She ran indoors. I followed her and bolted the door from the inside.

Thereafter I could not have enough of Ram Dulari. I could not take my eyes off her. Every movement she made fired me with desire to take her. Every moment I was away from her was a torment and I hurried back home to be in her embrace. And she became coquetish. 'Ajee, I am not a whore you can have anytime you like—not unless you pay me for it.' I bought her a nose-pin with a red ruby; I bought her glass bangles of all the colours I could find in the bazaar. For some months our world was narrowed to a small charpoy on which we sported night and day.

Ram Dulari and I became members of a community which worshipped both in Hindu temples and in Sufi hospices. We celebrated Hindu festivals as well as the Muslim. At Dassehra we went to see Ram Lila, on

Diwali we lit oil-lamps on the parapet of our house, at Holi we squirted coloured water on our Hindu friends. On Id we exchanged gifts with Muslims we knew; on the death anniversaries of Muslim saints we went to the mausoleum of Qutubuddin Bakhtiyar Kaki. And at least once a month we went to Ghiaspur and watched the sky at dusk to see if the new moon had risen.

Ram Dulari continued to dress as other Hindu women did. She wore crimson in the parting of her hair, a red dot on her forehead, and a mangalsutra (a necklace of black and gold beads.) I continued to dress like a Turk with a skull cap and turban. Like the Turks I sported a neatly trimmed beard and moustache. And I spoke the way they did. If they said 'As Salaam-Valai-kum' (peace be with you) I replied 'valai-kum-As-Salaam' (and with you too be peace.) If they asked me how I was, I replied 'Al-hamdu-illah' (well, by the grace of God.) But if they asked me 'Abdullah when will you become a true Muslim?' I would reply 'Soon, if that be the will of God—Inshallah.' If anyone asked me whether we were Hindus or Mussalmans, we would reply we were both. Nizamuddin was our umbrella against the burning sun of Muslim bigotry and the downpour of Hindu contempt.

So passed the days, weeks and months. By the end

of the year Ram Dulari was pregnant and had to go to her parents in Mathura for her confinement. When news of the birth of a son was brought to me I sent plates full of sweets to the Kotwal Sahib and to all our Muslim and Hindu friends. After a few weeks I went to Mathura to bring back my wife and son. Ram Dulari's sisters made a lot of fuss over me. They teased me, 'Are you going to have the boy circumcised? Are you going to name him Mohammed or Ali or something like that?' I let them say what they liked. I had great fun with them.

I did not have my son circumcised. I had his head shaved and got a Brahmin to recite mantras. I chose the name Kamal for him—it could be either Hindu or Muslim. In Hindi it meant the lotus flower. In Arabic, pronounced with a longer accent on the second 'a', it meant excellence. We took the child to Jogmaya temple and had the priest daub sandalpaste on his forehead. Then we took him to Ghiaspur and had the Khwaja Sahib bless him. I recorded my gratitude to my peer by having his name inscribed on stone as my benefactor and embedding the stone in the outer wall of our home.

THE ROOFTOP MASSAGE

It was Sunday. No office. I slept longer than usual. I picked up Molly, carried her to her room and tucked her into her own bed. 'Sleep as late as you like. It's Sunday. It will be a late breakfast—early brunch. Take your own time.'

She mumbled something I couldn't make out and turned over and went back to sleep.

I opened the front door, picked up the Sunday papers lying in a heap by the gate, and went back to my room. I switched on the electric radiator and got back into bed to read the papers. The bearer brought me tea. In half an hour I had run through the six papers and their colour supplements. There was nothing much to read. I went up to the roof to check the arrangements. The two rexine mattresses were lying next to each other, drenched in dew; I walked around the roof. It was higher than the roofs of the other houses.

I could see my neighbours; they could not see me. The rooftops were a forest of TV and dish antennae as far as the eyes could see. While strolling around in the chill morning, it occurred to me that I had missed out on my Surya Namaskar for many days. I stood facing the rising sun and went through all the motions. I felt the better for it.

I bathed, changed into a sports shirt and slacks and put on a thick sweater. Molly emerged from her room after ten, freshly bathed and in one of the salwar-kameez sets she had bought the day before. 'How do I look?' she asked, looking down at her long shirt.

'Very nice! I suggest you wrap a shawl around you. This weather can be very treacherous.'

She went back and came out with a hand-knitted woollen scarf that barely covered her front. We sat down in front of the electric radiator. I lit my cigar, she lit her cigarette.

'It promises to be a bright, sunny day. The mattresses are on the roof and I've got a bottle of herbal oil to put on my skin. We can sunbathe all afternoon till the sun goes down.'

'That will be lovely,' she replied.

We had a light brunch of hot Chinese sweet-and-sour soup and ham sandwiches. The servants cleared the table and left for their quarters.

'Come and take a look at the bandobast,' I said, and led her by the hand up the stairs to the roof. The sun was bright and warm. It had dried the dew on the mattresses. A bottle of herbal oil was warming itself in the sun. Molly walked round the roof to make sure that no one could see us.

'You get into a light dressing gown,' she ordered, suddenly very professional and in command, 'I'll get into my working clothes.'

We waited to let the sun get warmer.

When we went up again, it was exactly overhead. There was no breeze. 'Perfect for sunbathing,' pronounced Molly. 'Take off your dressing gown and lie down on your stomach.'

I did as I was ordered. She took off her cotton nightie and tossed it on the ground. She had not a stitch on her except the gold chain around her ankle. She came over and sat on my back—astride—as if riding a horse. I could feel her pubic hair tickle the base of my spine. With both her hands she kneaded my spine from bottom to top, over and over again. She pressed her thumbs hard into my shoulder blades, then twisted them, rinsing out all the tension. She filled her palms with warm herbal oil, smeared it on my back, and repeated the process: up the spinal cord, behind the neck to the base of the skull, round the ears, down to the shoulders and back to the base of the spine. She got up, stepped over me twice and again sat down on my back, this time facing my feet. She put more oil in her palms and went over my buttocks and between them, circling my anus lightly, then to my thighs, legs, ankles, down to every toe. This went on for almost half an hour. It was very soothing and sensuous. Every inch of my body was aching to be ministered to by her loving fingers. She stood above me and ordered, 'Turn around.'

I turned around and lay on my back. I got a worm's eye view of her thighs and what they concealed. She sat down on my stomach. She ran her fingers round my nipples. I had not realized a man's nipples could be as sensitive as a woman's. She poured oil on my chest and with open palms rubbed it into my torso many times. Once again she changed positions; now her buttocks were towards my face. As she stretched forward and back, her pubic hair grazed the line of hair running down from my navel to my groin. She slapped a liberal palmful of oil beneath my testicles and rubbed it into my inner thighs, down to the ankles and the feet. She had to lean forward to massage my feet and I had a splendid view of her anus and pubic fluff. I began to react. My penis sprang to full life and slapped against her thigh as it did so. She slapped it down and away. 'Patience!' she admonished.

The massage went on for an hour. I can't recall ever having experienced anything more pleasurable and sensual—even more than sexual intercourse. She wiped her oily hands against her sides and lay down on her mattress, face down. This time I went over and sat astride her, my balls caressing the small of her back as I moved. Though I had not massaged anyone before, I imitated her. I massaged her body from her neck to her toes, first the rear then the front. I glued my lips to her nipples in turn and slowly entered her. It was heavenly. I stayed inside her a long time, both of us motionless. Then I pulled out and asked her to turn around. She lay on her stomach with her legs wide apart, I positioned myself between her thighs and began to massage her buttocks. Come to think of it, a woman's buttocks excite a man more than any other part of her body— more than her lips or breasts or her pussy. And Molly's were beautifully rounded and firm. I found them irresistible and slowly entered her cunt from the rear.

She gave a long sigh of pleasure and let me go further and further into her. We did our best to prolong our bliss. Every time I felt I was coming I pulled out and sat still till the crisis had passed. Then we resumed our search for the ultimate truth of bodily existence: at times she pressed into me from above with my hands squeezing and pressing her buttocks to urge her on; then I on top, with her nails stuck into my posterior. When neither of us could hold out any longer, we went at each other like wild animals, tearing and clawing each other's flesh. The climax was the most prolonged that either of us had experienced in our lives.

No words were spoken. Words were superfluous. We lay on our mattresses and let the sun dry up the oil on our bodies. We had been at it for almost three hours.

After worshipping the sun with our bodies in our own unique way, we went downstairs to cleanse ourselves of the oil on them. I fetched two loofahs and gave her one to run over her limbs after she had soaped herself. There is nothing better than a loofah to scrape oil or dirt off one's body. I felt cleaner than ever before. I got into my woollen dressing gown, switched on the electric radiator and lit a cigar. Molly joined me a few minutes later and lit a cigarette.

'That was heavenly,' I said. 'Don't you think so?'

'Never known anything better in my life,' she replied with a smile. 'But let's not try to repeat it.'

'Why on earth not?'

'This kind of lovemaking, in which every part of your body makes love to every part of your partner's, is a once-in-a-lifetime experience. Dwell on it in your mind, never try to relive it in action. It will be a great disappointment.'

BUGGERED

It all started during my recent summer vacation in Kasauli. I woke up one night with a queasy feeling in my stomach. Half asleep, I tottered to the loo to rid myself of my sleep-breaker. When I got up from the lavatory seat to flush the contents, I was shocked to see I had passed a lot of blood with my stool. 'Shit!' I said to myself, suddenly wide awake. The rest of the night was wasted in contemplation of the end. I had had a reasonable innings, close to scoring a century, so no regrets on that score. Was I creating a self-image of heroism in the face of death? That vanished on the following day as more blood flowed out of my belly.

I asked my friend, Dr Santosh Kutty of the Central Research Institute (CRI), to drop in for a drink in the evening. Over a glass of Scotch, he heard me out. When I finished, he asked me: 'Have you been eating chukandar?' I admitted I'd had beetroot salad the day before.

'It could be that,' he suggested. 'It is the same colour as human blood. Or it could be nature's way of reducing high blood pressure—bleeding through the nose or arse. Or it could be a polyp, or piles, or...' He did not use the word but I understood he meant cancer. 'Let me examine your rectum.'

'You'll do no such thing,' I rasped. 'I'd rather die than show my rectum to anyone.' He paused, and continued, 'It would be wise to have an enteroscopy. It will clear all doubts. We don't have the facility in Kasauli. You can have it done at PGI in Chandigarh or in Delhi. The sooner the better.'

I opted for Delhi, to be with my family. And rang up my friend Nanak Kohli to send up his Mercedes Benz to take me down.

I looked up my dictionary to find out exactly what polyp and enteroscopy meant. One is a kind of sea urchin-like growth in the lower part of the intestine, the other an instrumental examination of one's innards. I spent the rest of the day drafting in my mind farewell letters to my near and dear ones. Nothing mawkish or sentimental, but in the tone of one who couldn't care less about his fate, something they could quote in my obituaries: he went like a man, with a smile on his face, etc., etc.

The next morning, my son, Rahul, and I drove back to Delhi.

The first thing I did was to ask Dr I.P.S. Kalra, who lives in the neighbouring block, to come over. Dr Kalra is a devout believer in miracles performed by Wahe Guru. He has been our doctor for over half a century and has treated several members of my extended family in their last days on earth, until their journey to the electric crematorium. Since I am a lot older than him, he addresses me as Veerjee (elder brother). He took my blood pressure, it was higher than normal. He heard my bloody tale and straightaway fixed an appointment with Dr S.K. Jain, Delhi's leading endoscopist.

The next evening, accompanied by Kalra, Rahul and my daughter, Mala, I presented myself at Dr Jain's swanky clinic in Hauz Khas Enclave. All white marble, spotlessly clean, and with the obligatory statuette of Lord Ganapati, with a garland of fresh marigold flowers around his neck, sitting above the receptionist's desk. Since I was the first patient of the many he had to examine that evening, I was conducted immediately to his operating room.

I can tell you that enteroscopy strips your self-esteem and any dignity you may have. I was ordered to take off my salwar kameez, given an overall to wear, and ordered to lie down. Dr Jain took my blood pressure and proceeded to insert an endoscope up my rectum. At times the pain was excruciating. It went on for an hour. When it was over, Dr Kalra ordered me, 'Veerjee, pudd maro—kill a fart, you'll feel easier.' I refused to oblige and instead went to the lavatory to get rid of the wind the nervous tension had created inside me.

Dr Jain pronounced the verdict: 'No polyp, no cancer, only internal piles which bleed because of high BP. It is nature's way of bringing it down.' As a parting gift, he gave Mala a filmed version of all that had transpired— from my bottom being bared to the muck inside my belly. As if that was not enough, when asked about his father's health, Rahul told everyone, 'Pop has piles.' There is something romantic about cancer; polyp is like a plop sound produced by a frog leaping into a stagnant pool; but haemorrhoids have no romance attached to them; they are simply a miserable man's piles. Many well-wishers called to enquire how my enteroscopy had gone and how I felt about the whole exercise. My reply was standard: 'I feel buggered.'

ACKNOWLEDGEMENTS

The literary estate of Khushwant Singh and the publishers gratefully acknowledge Penguin Books India for permission to reprint the following copyright material:

'My First Love in College' and 'England Days, and Losing My Virginity', both of which have been adapted from *Truth, Love and a Little Malice: An Autobiography*; 'A Mixed Marriage', adapted from *Delhi: A Novel*; and 'The Rooftop Massage', taken from *The Company of Women*.